THE AUTHORITARIAN REGIME SURVIVAL GUIDE

Text by
Martin Mycielski

Introduction by
Ric Kasini Kadour

Artwork by
Heather Wright
Lori Petchers
Olivia Baldacci
Suzanne Gore
Andrea Lee
Heather Wishik
Jennifer R Myhre

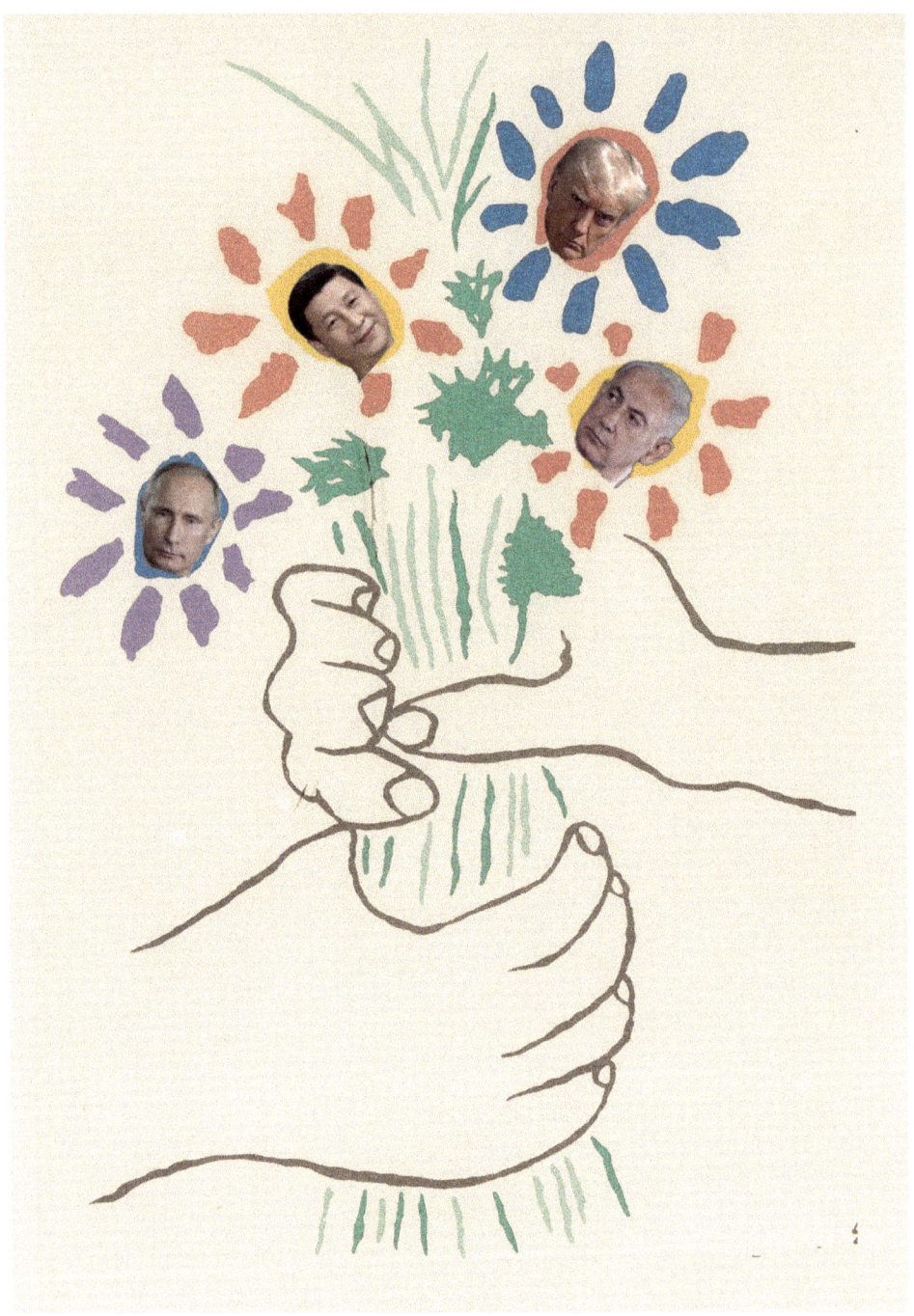

Bouquet of Dictators by Suzanne Gore

Suzanne Gore collages faces of world leaders into Pablo Picasso's 1958 lithograph, *The Flowers of Peace*, which he made in honor of the International Peace Conference taking place in Stockholm that year. "While it may seem to many current viewers that fascist regimes occurred in another lifetime, it is actually less than a century ago," wrote the artist. "I want the contrast of war, genocide and the ruthless destruction of human rights to be a striking contrast in a *Bouquet of Peace*." The leaders from left to right are Vladimir Putin (Russia), Xi Jinping (China), Donald Trump (USA), and Benjamin Netanyahu (Israel).

CONTENTS

7
INTRODUCTION

29
UNDER AUTHORITARIANISM
WHAT TO EXPECT

63
AUTHORITARIAN CHECKLIST

67
SIX RULES FOR SURVIVAL
UNDER AN AUTHORITARIAN REGIME

81
SEVEN RULES ON APPROACHING
AUTHORITARIAN SUPPORTERS

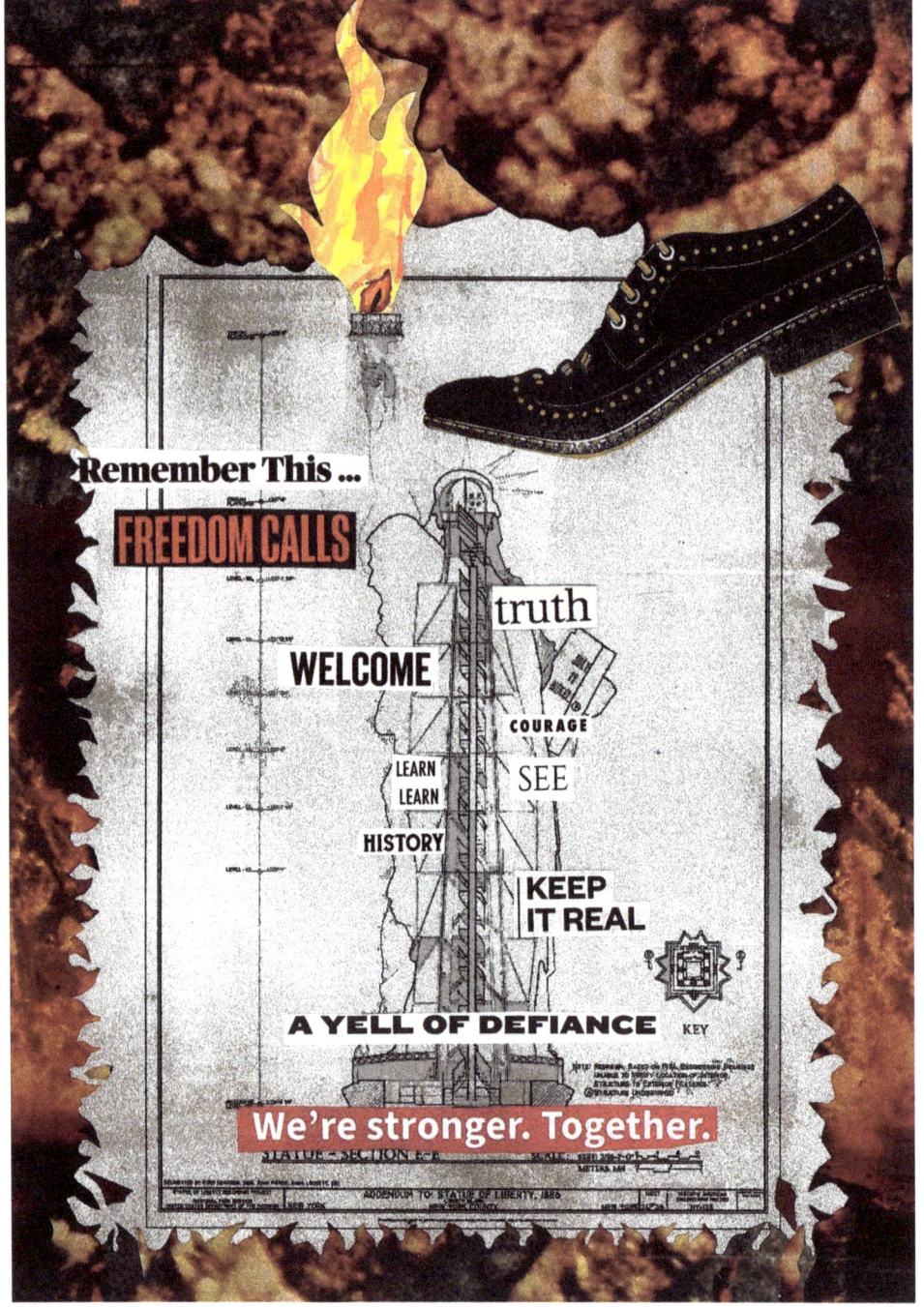

What Is Liberty Made Of? by Jennifer R Myhre

What are the inner workings of freedom? A cross sectional diagram of the Statue of Liberty asks us to consider the foundations of democratic society. Authoritarian regimes co-opt, distort, or negate national symbols as a way to take power in a free society. Myhre's collage reminds us that these symbols—and their original meanings—are ideas worth protecting and fighting for.

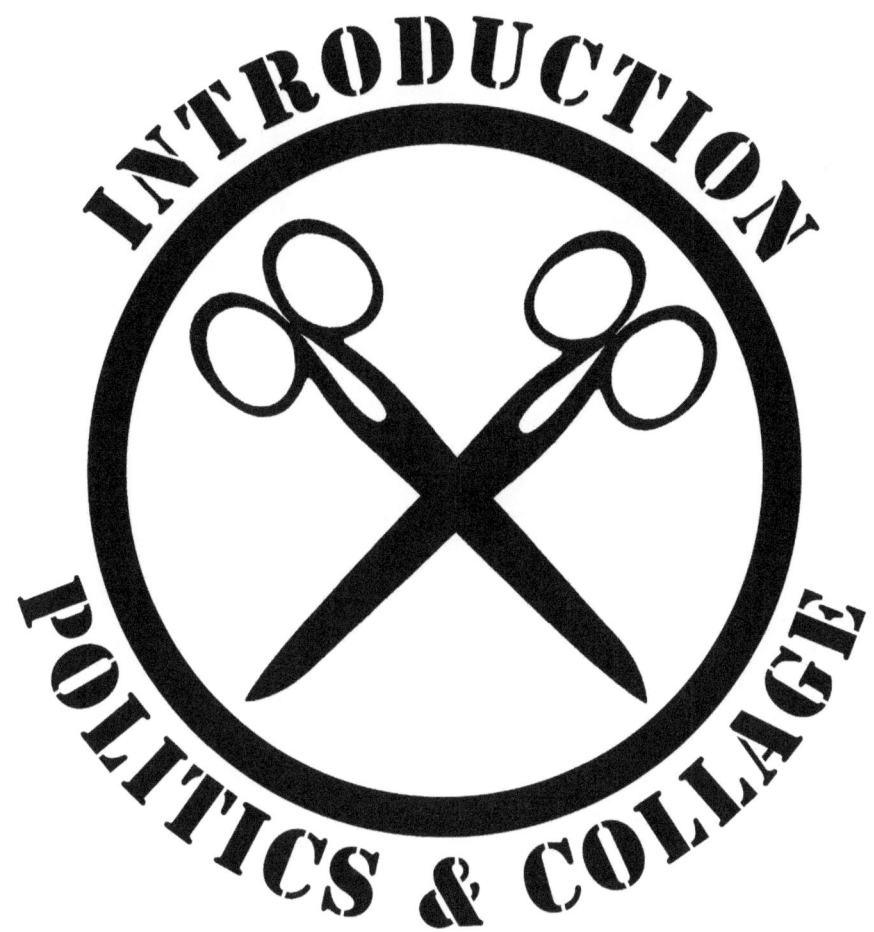

ower, or the ability to influence the actions, beliefs, and thinking of others, is a complex web of forces that shapes our understanding of the world and our place in it. Power is an ecosystem, a thousand moving parts, informed by physical and perceived realities of our psychological, cultural, social, and physical existence. Power has a history, changes overtime, is in a constant state of renegotiation, and yet, feels ahistorical, transcendental. In "Society Must Be Defended", the French philosopher Michel Foucault wrote, "Power functions. Power is exercised through networks, and individuals do not simply circulate in those networks; they are in a position to both submit to and exercise this power. They are never the inert or consenting targets of power; they are always its relays. In other words, power passes through individuals. It is not applied to them."[1]

In 5th century BCE Greek city-states, thinkers made a distinction between a democracy where decisions were made collectively by the people and an aristocracy where decisions were made by a ruling elite. Throughout history, notions of citizenship (who was consid-

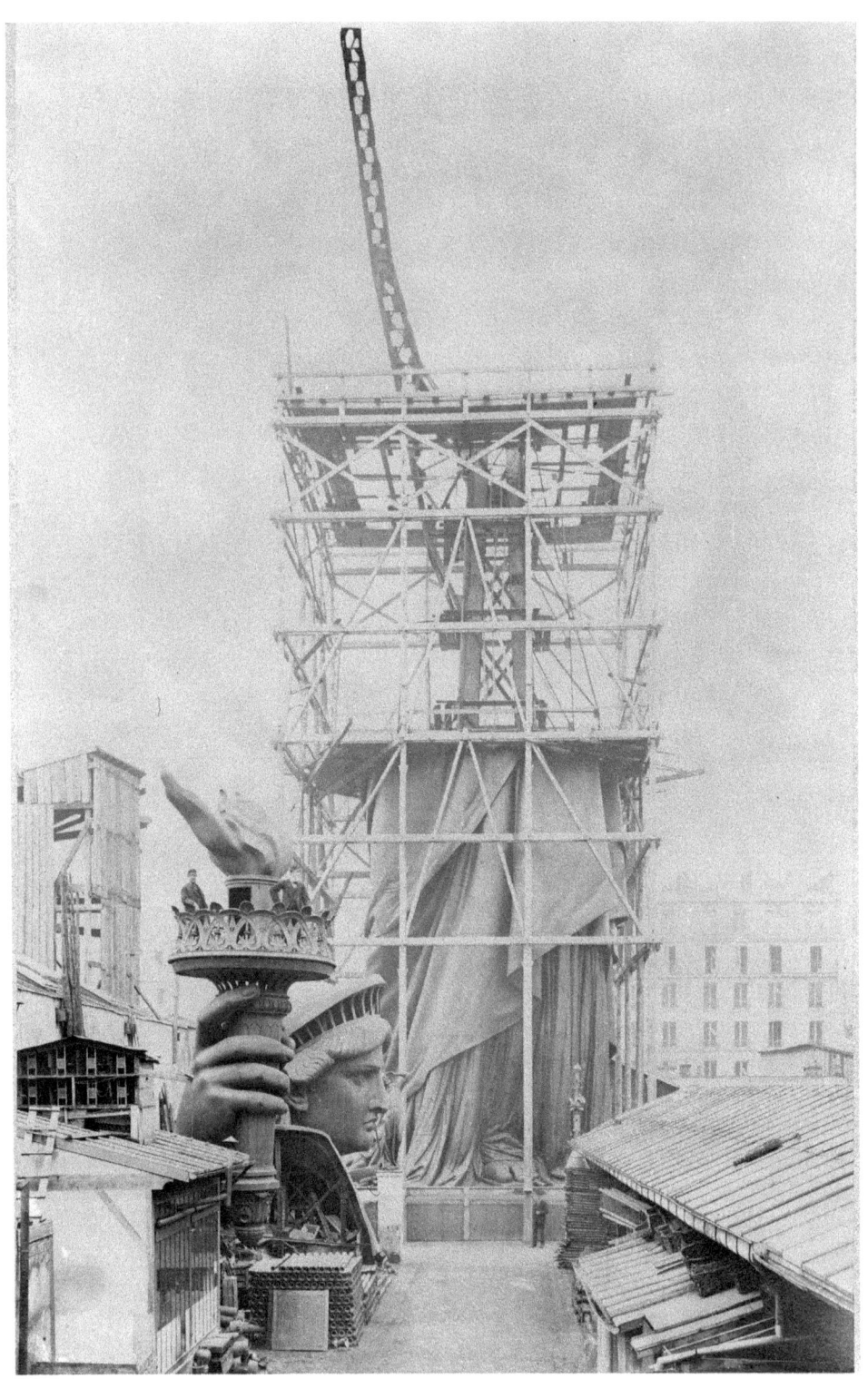

Assemblage of the Statue of Liberty in Paris, showing the bottom half of the statue erect under scaffolding, the head and torch at its feet by Albert Fernique (photograph; 1883. The New York Public Library Photography Collection, 1161037.)

ered a member of the state) and suffrage (who had the right to participate in the decision making process) were constantly being negotiated. Even in monarchical autocracies, those in power were dependent on a constituency that allowed them to be so. Throughout history, humanity has experimented with democracy: from the Vajjika League in India in the 6th century BCE to the 12th century Haudenosaunee of the Iroquois confederacy to the Golden Liberty of 16th century Poland and so on. The democracy created in 1787 by the United States with its codified constitution, grounding in the rule of law, separation of powers, and the idea of an elected government tasked with protecting civil rights and liberties was, while imperfect, exceptional in its ability to evolve over time; to expand those rights and liberties and to work towards "a more perfect union," words stated in the preamble of its founding document.

American democracy is so exceptional that the thought of it not existing, of it not correcting its imperfections, is anathema to America's sense of itself. So much so that when filmmakers want to show the end of humanity, they often show The Statue of Liberty, a symbol of American democracy, as destroyed, damaged, or partially buried. Americans in particular struggle to imagine a world without the rights and privileges afforded them by their government and when they travel outside of their country sometimes assume those same rights travel with them, often leading to tragic or comedic outcomes. This is because systems of power are ecological, almost cosmological in nature. When working, they are invisible and they feel like the natural order of things. But what happens when they change, when freedom is eroded, when democracy collapses into authoritarianism?

This is a difficult conversation to have because talking about the end of democracy, the end of freedom, looks and feels like the ramblings of lunatics. The collective historical reference for the rise of authoritarianism is the rise of the Nazi party in early 20th century Germany, but that history has been so bandied about, quoted and misquoted, that it has become almost like folklore. Few appreciate the slow, incremental drip into authoritarianism that took place over decades. A lot of democracy took place between the Beer Hall Putsch (8 November 1923) to Hitler being appointed Chancellor of Germany (30 January 1933) and the Reichstag Fire (27 February 1933) and passage of the Law Against the Formation of Parties (14 July 1933) and Night of the Long Knives (30 June 1934) and the Invasion of Poland (1 September 1939). Dachau concentration camp opened on 22 March 1933. As early as 1935, Germans had sayings about it: "Lieber Herr Gott, mach mich stumm, dass ich nicht nach Dachau komm" ("Dear Lord God, make me dumb, That I may not to Dachau come"). Christopher Isherwood, in his first-hand account of living in Germany during this period, *Goodbye to Berlin*, published in 1939, does not show a society grappling with the rise of authoritarianism but a people eking out an existence under difficult economic circumstances. They are worried about paying their rent or the price of food or whether their children will find a job; the banality of life. We think of history as a series of events but in reality, history is a slow evolution. By 1945, one out of every nine Germans would be dead, more than half at the hands of their own government.

This book is a collage. It combines the text of a Polish human rights activist with the artwork of seven collage artists. Collectively, we hope to create a space in which we can think about the rise of authoritarianism and how to navigate the troubling, difficult times in which we find ourselves. This book is also a document of the role art can play in society. In this introduction, I hope to share the history of the project and offer some critical context and analysis of the artworks; to share some thoughts about how authoritarianism operates culturally and what political art does and does not do.

This book came about in three ways.

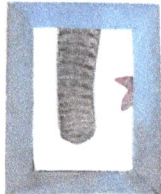

First. In 2017, Martin Mycielski, the Vice-President and Executive Director of the Brussels-based Open Dialogue Foundation, published a series of improvised, spontaneous tweets that became *The Authoritarian Regime Survival Guide* after they went viral and reached 3 million views within one month. With a background working for the European Parliament, Mycielski was one of the founders of Komitet Obrony Demokracji (or KOD, Committee for the Defense of Democracy) in response to the 2015 constitutional crisis in Poland. He also co-founded the EU DisinfoLab, "the first European NGO committed strictly to countering disinformation," and served as the Brussels correspondent for *Gazeta Wyborcza*, the leading Polish daily newspaper.[2]

Mycielski found himself reflecting on his experience protesting the government's actions during the 2015 constitutional crisis as Donald Trump was being sworn into office in January 2017. Mycielski recalled how the text came about:

It was Saturday night. I couldn't fall asleep. I had all of these experiences fighting the illiberal government in Poland. We had this huge, huge, huge uprising of street protest movements with all of these activists and organizations springing up. Of course, I was part of that. I saw what was happening in the US. I saw Trump's election and the direction that he said that he would go in. We know, of course, that many of those, let's say, threats/promises didn't materialize. I was very active on social media, mostly Twitter. I saw the reaction of civil society, of Americans from all walks of life. Everyone was panicking. I saw people looking for guidance, looking for examples from other parts of the world. What do you do in a situation like that? What do you do when an autocrat suddenly takes power? When your democracy is threatened, when the rule of law is threatened, how do you react?

I had a simple, gut reaction: "Guys, we've been going through this for the last two years. Let me share our experiences with you." I started with a series of tweets.

Several ideas came to mind. First, what happened exactly? I tried to remember the specific steps that this government took to come to power and how they were expanding that power. I tried to describe it and then our reaction to it, how civil society responded to all those threats. There were several parts to the guide. It was never finalized or published in a complete form; but, it was more or less relevant to the situation back then. I would definitely change some things now, seeing how everything unfolded over the following six years. Still, I think that my recommendations and my diagnosis of the situation back then was correct.

It was spontaneous. It was never planned. To be clear, I had no expertise. I was a citizen, like everyone else. I was among tens, hundreds of thousands of Polish people who were looking for ways to react to what was happening, to somehow stop it from happening.[3]

Mycielski signed his tweets, "With Love from Your Eastern European Friends" and used the hashtag #LearnFromEurope. "The Guide went viral in the US and many other countries, being translated into several languages, from Turkish to Filipino. It was printed on placards during anti-Trump protests, studied at two American universities, quoted by CNBC's Joy Reid on national TV and recommended by former US Secretary of Labor Robert Reich." In March 2018, *Verfassungsblog*, "a global forum of scholarly debate at the interface of academy and society," published the text in its entirety.[4]

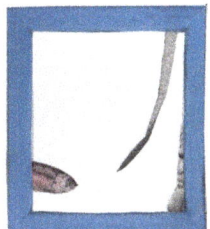

Second. After the election of Donald Trump in November 2024, I found myself with a nagging anxiety about America's future. On the one hand, we survived the first Trump administration. While I had hoped the putting of children in cages (June 2018); the bumbled management of the COVID-19 Pandemic; the series of Hatch Act and Emoluments Clause Violations; the interference in the Department of Justice; the insurrection at the U.S. Capitol (January 2021) or the daily whiplash of absurdity would have exasperated America's indulgence for a self-declared wannabe dictator, apparently the country wanted a second run at the trough. To be honest, I had stopped caring about Donald Trump a while ago. For me, the current state of affairs is the product of forty years of slow boiling to this moment; an evolution in the system of power that started with Ronald Reagan and has percolated in the decades since. I had expatriated myself once already, leaving for Canada when George W. Bush was reelected in 2004.

A queer man who came of age during the AIDS epidemic, while there have been glimmers of hope, I have felt since the 1990s that America has lost the ability to fix itself. As a culture worker interested in history and our civic discourse, I am less concerned with the news of the day than I am the social forces that make that news possible. I am more interested in who humanity will be a decade or a generation from now and how we use the past to imagine those possibilities. In spite of trying to hold on to a long-term view, in the months after the 2024 election, I found myself anxious about and making plans for the worst case scenario: daily physical violence against the people I care about. These were familiar feelings and reminded me of silly dreams of Karl Rove putting queer people on buses to concentration camps back in 2004 that led me to move to Canada. At times of political, societal upheaval, it is hard to distinguish between rational caution and paranoid lunacy. In that moment, I remembered Mycielski's 2017 social media campaign and found the text on *Verfassungsblog*.

On 7 November 2024, I sent Mycielski an email. "I would like to build an Artist Lab around *The Authoritarian Regime Survival Guide* and invite artists to make artwork that animates the ideas expressed within. The results would be an exhibition at our gallery in New Orleans, Louisiana, USA, a folio of artwork available for a traveling exhibition, and a small publication." Mycielski replied ten minutes later, "Thanks for reaching out. I did notice that—for obvious and grim reasons—my old guide has seen a resurgence since yesterday. Of course, I'd be honored to have my work featured in such a unique, creative project. Happy to speak about its history, too." We were off and running.[5]

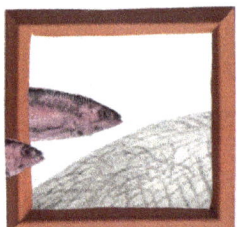

Third. Kolaj Institute exists to support artists, curators, and writers who seek to study, document, and disseminate ideas that deepen our understanding of collage as a medium, a genre, a community, and a 21st century movement. We operate a number of initiatives meant to bring together community, investigate critical issues, and raise the standing of collage in the art world. Our philosophy is that if we bring artists together, explore ideas and concepts, share knowledge, we can stretch and develop as artists. When we bring that knowledge and skill into our communities, we raise the standing of collage and contribute to the civic discourse.

In "Empty Columns Are a Place to Dream" (2021), we bought together eighteen artists from eleven countries to use the photograph, *The Square, Parsonstown* by Robert French (1841-1917) from the Lawrence Photograph Collection in Birr, County Offaly, Ireland, to imagine a monument that speaks to a world where all people enjoy safety, security, well-being, and dignity on their own terms. For "Artists in the Archives" (2022), we worked with an international network of collage artists to engage with historic material in the Stewart-Swift Research Center archive at the Henry Sheldon Museum of Vermont History to create a folio of collage prints that reflect on the idea of community in a 21st century world. A program centered on collage and illustration takes vintage, public domain stories and recontextualizes them for a 21st century audience with collaborative collage illustrations.

Since 2021, "Politics in Collage" has been a series of residencies, publications, discus-

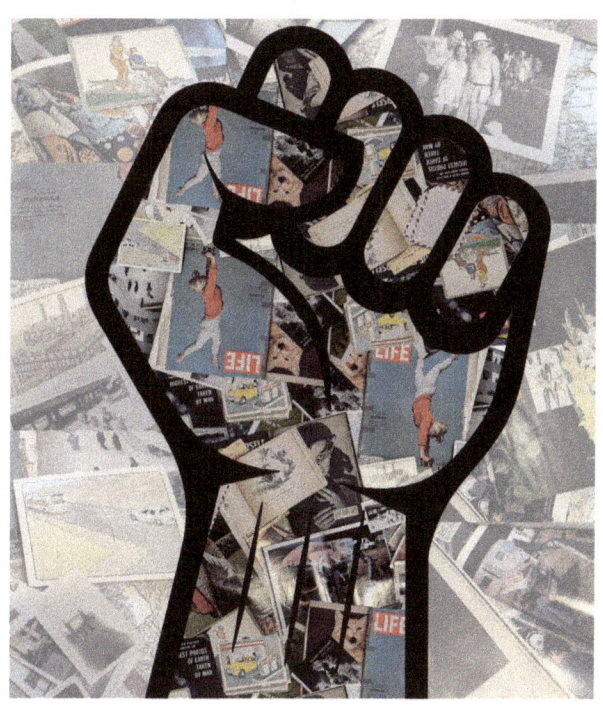

Politics in Collage graphic by Ric Kasini Kadour (2024)

sions, and exhibitions examining complex socio-political issues with which contemporary society contends, in order to spark meaningful dialogue and inspire deeper engagement. We wrote articles on how collage was used to visualize the 2019-2021 Estallido Social in Chile, which incidentally birthed a new collage community. We published books and organized exhibitions that came out of residencies led by G.E. Vogt and Christopher Kurts where guest speakers like John Heartfield, Jr. presented his grandfather's artwork and spoke about how he used collage to resist Adolf Hitler's control of Germany.

I felt confident that we could bring artists together and make collage that would be in conversation with the text of Mycielski's *Authoritarian Regime Survival Guide*. Ten artists joined the virtual residency we organized. It started on 19 January 2025, the day before the Inauguration of Trump's second term. I hoped this would be a project in which I and other artists could part with unfounded anxieties about the new administration, to use the present moment to explore political collage and that even if the new administration failed to enact their agenda, we would have made artwork that spoke about the larger global rise of authoritarianism documented by Freedom House and the general struggle for democracy that had been taking place around the world for a century.

"When I talk about the times we are in," I said to the artists in our first meeting. "I am holding space for the immediate now but also the broader trend that has been going on with the rise of authoritarianism and the move to the right that we have seen over the past few

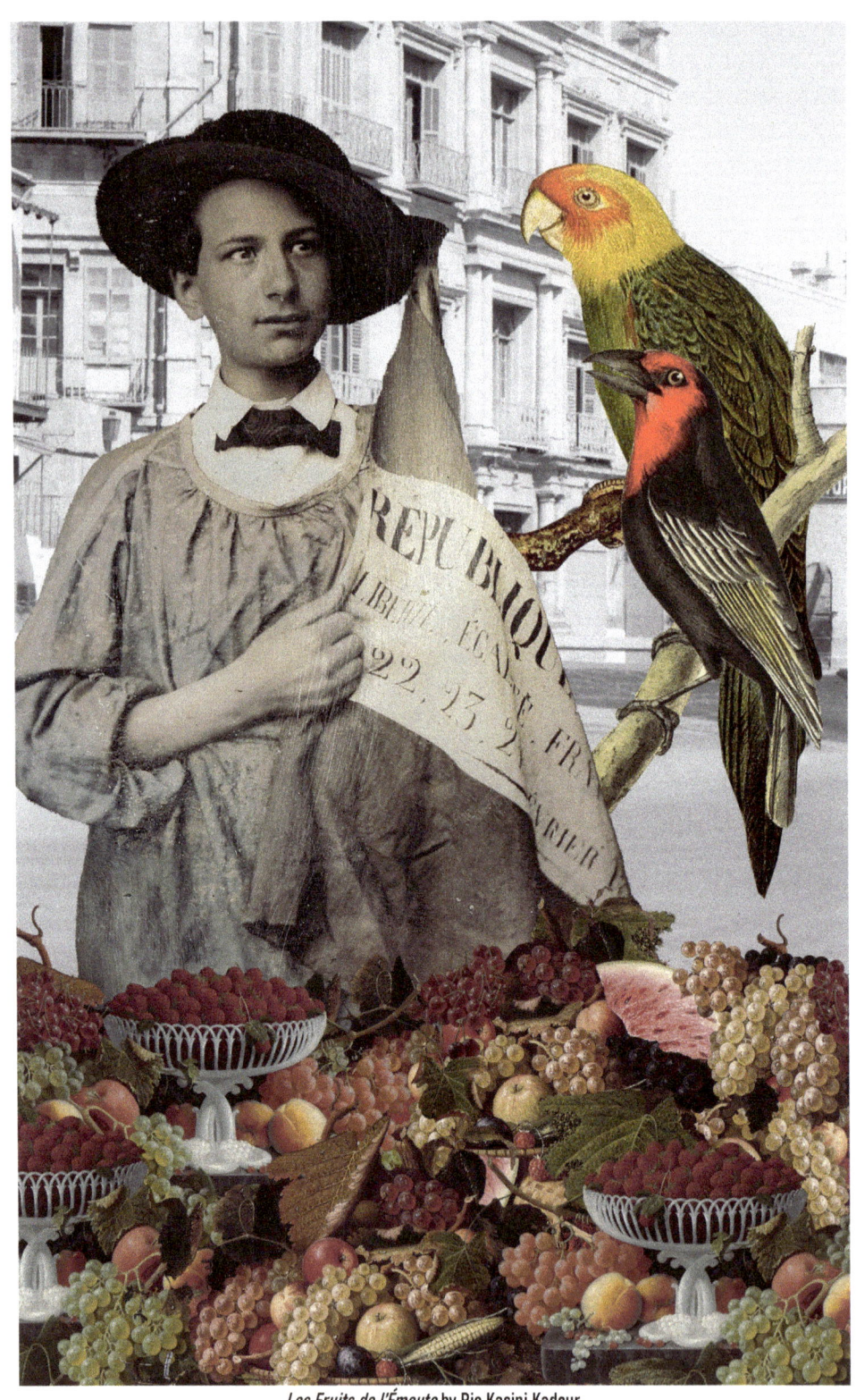

Les Fruits de l'Émeute by Ric Kasini Kadour
collage print, 2025

years. Also, I want to hold space for—even though most of us are Americans or thinking about America right now—this as a global issue. The collage community is an international one and we see what has been happening on every continent. To do this work, we will explore the idea of Political Art: How do we use collage to speak to difficult socio-political topics? How do we bring complexity and nuance to issues that are presented as black and white, right and wrong, moral absolutes? How can we make art that picks up the unfinished work of history and contributes to the civic discourse? Those are our challenges."[6]

I grounded the project in the 2022 report, *Freedom in the World* published by Washington, DC-based Freedom House, "the oldest American organization devoted to the support and defense of democracy around the world...[which] was formally established in New York in 1941 to promote American involvement in World War II and the fight against fascism."[7] Authors Sarah Repucci and Amy Slipowitz wrote, "Around the world, the enemies of liberal democracy—a form of self government in which human rights are recognized and every individual is entitled to equal treatment under law—are accelerating their attacks. Authoritarian regimes have become more effective at co-opting or circumventing the norms and institutions meant to support basic liberties, and at providing aid to others who wish to do the same. In countries with long-established democracies, internal forces have exploited the shortcomings in their systems, distorting national politics to promote hatred, violence, and unbridled power."[8]

I asked the group, "What can collage artists do to counter rising authoritarianism?" I also told the group, "Depending on where you are in society, who you are in society, some of this isn't new. Some of us have been sitting with and wrestling with these ideas all of our lives. It's important to hold and acknowledge space for that."

I also spoke about what we didn't want. "What we're interested in is NOT making posters. There's a place for posters and banners. We're interested in making art that gets deeper at the issues. In that sense, I think there is an urgency in terms of our own art practices. Who are we now and how are we operating and being in the world." I shared with the artists a conversation with an equally aged activist artist I met last summer. "We were bemoaning turning fifty and it felt like we've been saying the same shit over and over and it's exhausting. We landed on this place; we're too old to get tear gassed. We've done it and we don't want to do it again. I'm too old to go to the street. What is my role now? We had this helpful conversation on the role of seed planting, the role of thinking about what can I do now that someone in ten years can find and remember the moment. What can I do now that might inspire someone to go to the street? We still need people to go to the street. I want this book to be as relevant in ten years or twenty years as it may be in two months."

I recalled the history of early 20th century Berlin and the freedom queer people experienced and how quickly it went away. "Power needs amnesia. Power needs us to forget that we were in a better place before. Power needs us to forget past atrocities. That is why the Black history of America becomes so relevant because it reminds us of how hostile power can be. As artists, we can find ways to speak to that amnesia." I asked the artists to consider the relationship between art and time. "Art always operates in the future. If you make an art today, it is not going to be seen until tomorrow. It's not going to make its way into the world for another month or two. It's not going to be thought about until it is out in the world being seen and reflected on. That is not happening when you make it, that is happening in the future."

We considered the work of German visual artist, John Heartfield, who pioneered the use of art as a political weapon. Collage was integral to his practice. We looked at *Tool in God's Hand? Toy in Thyssen's Hand!*, a satirization of Hitler and the Nazi regime that shows industrialist Fritz Thyssen holding a Hitler puppet. In this work, Heartfield connects business interests with the pursuit of political power. We also looked at a version of *Krieg! (Niemals wieder!) (Der Sinn von Genf. Wo das Kapital lebt, kann der Friede nicht leben!)* (War! (Never again!) (The Meaning of Geneva. Where Capital lives, Peace cannot live!)) that showed a bayonet piercing a white dove. This artwork was originally made in 1932 as a reminder to German society about the brutality of war. Heartfield reworked this image in 1942 from London and as a 1959 poster in East Germany. At each incarnation of *Krieg! (Niemals wieder!)*, Heartfield was trying to counter the forced amnesia taking place.

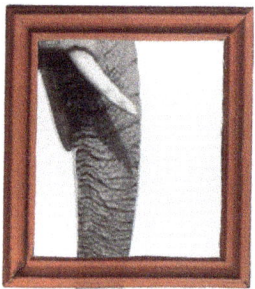

Nearly a century after Heartfield made his political collage, they stand as examples of how artists can use humor, satire, and deeply emotional imagery to speak to contemporary issues. They invite us to consider the rise of Authoritarianism as a historic and predictable pattern. These connections help viewers make sense of current events and provide tools to navigate an economic and political landscape that may feel novel. These artworks also invite us to contemplate issues of morality as they encourage us to consider what side of history we are on.

Krieg! (Niemals wieder!) inspired Fenelon Falls, Ontario, Canada artist Andrea Lee to make *Lettuce Not Waver*, a humorous parody of Heartfield's artwork that has a serious purpose. Lee wrote, "Nowhere is there a battlefield such as there was in Heartfield's time, least of all one where there is hand-to-hand combat. A plastic kitchen knife is used in place of a sword as a commentary on how close to home the issues of authoritarianism have become." As of this writing, the rise of authoritarianism has primarily had dramatic economic impacts; in Canada, in particular, where the cost of groceries has skyrocketed. Lee continued, "*Lettuce Not Waver* portrays a sense of *déjà vu,* a feeling of 'here we are again' at the tip of the knife, in danger from the threat of authoritarianism, like our Eastern European friends experienced not so long ago. Birds taking off in various trajectories seem to indicate prior knowledge. Unlike the single dove in the 1932 image, these birds saw things coming in time to take off, having had more than enough of violent human affairs. The shape and drape of the lettuce leaves memorializes the 1932 bird and reminds us of the violence that may yet to come, that there is much at stake, and that we should not waver in our commitment to stand strong."

Throw Out the Trash by Boise, Idaho, USA artist Suzanne Gore operates in a manner similar to Heartfield's *Tool in God's Hand?*. The two-bit collage puts Donald Trump's mug-shot into a vintage *LIFE* magazine advertisement. Ridicule of authoritarian figures is an important act of resistance. The audience here is not the person being satirized, rather it is to communicate to the community that the authoritarian is not morally acceptable nor as powerful as they may want to project. Gore wrote, "This work speaks to Trump's onslaught of unconstitutional and extreme executive orders along with the opinions spewed at his MAGA rallies and follows Mycielski's: Year 1 Under Authoritarianism What to Expect?—almost to the letter. It illustrates the opinion that the ideas and executive orders being hurled at and forced upon the people of the US and the world are garbage and should be taken out with the trash. The garbage in the bag represents the creation of chaos by the new-again administration. I want the viewer to see the rise in authoritarianism as something to bag and toss out—as necessary as taking out the trash."

Elgin, Minnesota, USA artist Heather Wright's *PU a Coup* is an extension of this work by equating the rise of authoritarianism with the smell of dead fish. Fairfield, Connecticut, USA artist Lori Petchers' *Gutting Justice* makes visceral the idea that authoritarian regimes "disembowel our legal system."

Collage artists are making meaning through their choice of material. Woodstock, Vermont, USA artist Heather Wishik wrote about making the collage, *They Will Create Chaos*, "This emerged from [my] play with saved materials. I saw the hand with the lightning bolts emerging from the fingers in my collection of magazine papers. The rest evolved as I sorted through my papers. The bullet hole in the Capitol window and the bombs indicate danger. The person trying to read with pages flying around suggests chaos, book banning and censorship. The hand with the lightning bolt suggests chaos created...The bombs suggest warmongering. Rainbow flags suggest the anti-LGBTQ policies of authoritarians including Victor Orban, Putin and Trump/Musk, and how these are framed as protective of children and parents." In collage, material is never neutral and collage artists are purposely appropriating and remixing culture. Like Lee's *Lettuce Never Waver*, Gore's *Bouquet of Dictators* draws from art history, specifically, Pablo Picasso's 1958 lithograph, *The Flowers of Peace*. In doing this, she is drawing a line between the right and wrong side of history and asking us to think about global leaders who are taking us down authoritarian paths. Gore is also inviting us to learn about the 1958 International Peace Conference in Stockholm and to think about the current state of affairs in the context of Cold War history. What lessons do we need to remember? What histories are we repeating?

Early in our group discussions, we decided that the artwork made for the project would not simply be an illustration of Mycielski's text, but rather a complement to it. This gave the artists free rein to draw from a variety of sources. Still, some artists made artwork in direct response to Mycielski's text. Gore's *Loyalties* speaks to the warning in What to Expect #3 about how authoritarians subjugate the media and limit press freedom. Wishik's *Ruining the Economy* is a direct illustration of What to Expect #14 which speaks to how authoritarians alienate trading partners while claiming not to need them. Wishik manipulated images from *The Economist* hoping "to stimulate viewers to register the deadly impact of an authoritarian meltdown of the US, and its economy, on the world."

Artists responded to current events. Wright's *Ingrates* was made in response to the contentious 28 February 2025 meeting between Donald Trump, JD Vance, and Volodymyr Zelenskyy in the Oval Office. Wishik's portrayal of the Statue of Liberty performing a Sieg Heil salute in *No Entry* is informed by Elon Musk's actions at the Capital One Arena during Trump's Second Inauguration. Wright's *No Worries* responds to early media articles about the administration's mass deportations.

Other artworks pull from specific histories. New York, New York, USA artist Olivia Baldacci worked with photographic documentation of The Bracero Program. The Library of Congress explained the program. "An executive order called the Mexican Farm Labor Program established the Bracero Program in 1942. This series of diplomatic accords between Mexico and the United States permitted millions of Mexican men to work legally in the United States on short-term labor contracts. These agreements addressed a national agricultural labor shortage during WWII and implicitly, they redressed previous depression-era deportations and repatriations that unjustly targeted Mexican Americans who were U.S. citizens."[9] An image at the center of the collage, *nostalgia (gasoline baths)*, is a 1956 Leonard Nadel photograph of Bracero workers being fumigated with the pesticide DDT in Hidalgo, Texas, from the collection of the National Museum of American History. This uncomfortable, but little known, part of American history is critical context for understanding the current discourse around the role of immigrant labor and the experiences of Latin American immigrants.

While unrecognizable on its surface, the fist in Petchers' *Truth and Dare* is taken from a photograph of Miss Montana, Kathy Huppe, published in the 18 September 1970 issue of *LIFE* magazine. Huppe was punished for speaking out against the Vietnam War and racial injustice. The use of this material in a subtle nod to remember this history and to apply its lessons to what we are experiencing today.

Sedona, Arizona, USA artist Jennifer R Myhre's *Who Is Watching the Watchers?* uses images from U.S. Military Intelligence files the artist photographed at the National Archives for a documentary about the federal government's surveillance and propaganda campaign against progressive movements in the early 20th century. She noted, "J. Edgar Hoover's COINTELPRO (1956-1971) program was the continuation of the Military Intelligence surveillance of labor organizers, civil rights organizers and feminists during this period." The

Federal Bureau of Investigation wrote that the program was "expanded to include a number of other domestic groups, such as the Ku Klux Klan, the Socialist Workers Party, and the Black Panther Party... COINTELPRO was later rightfully criticized by Congress and the American people for abridging first amendment rights and for other reasons."[10] Myhre's collage uses this history to remind us of the relationship between surveillance and authoritarianism.

In a healthy, progressive democracy, these artworks would invite us to sit with uncomfortable histories as a way to develop a sense of empathy and justice. The artwork may invite us to engage in a process of truth and reconciliation, to work towards a more fair and just society. But in the context of rising authoritarianism, this artwork is political defiance of the willful amnesia power demands we embrace. This is important culture work. Authoritarianism never lasts and its tenure and the recovery from it depends on our ability to remember what happened before and to return to the work of building a healthy society.

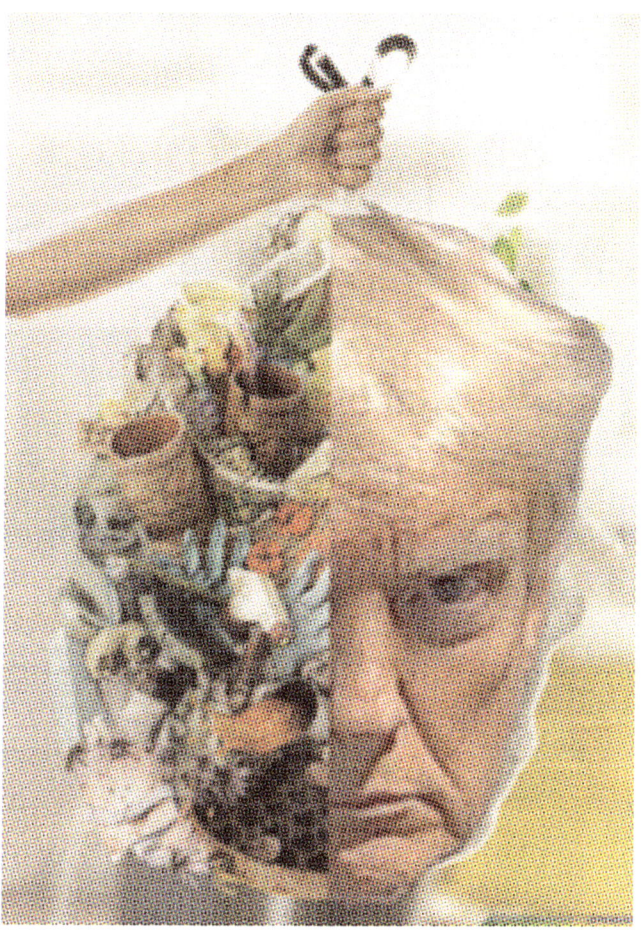

Throw Out The Trash by Suzanne Gore is an example of how artists satirize authoritarian figures.

Myhre's *Specific Suggestions for Simple Sabotage* continues this practice of using the U.S. Government's own archive materials to comment on authoritarianism and how to respond to it. Myhre cuts and pastes the declassified 1944 manual *Simple Sabotage Field Manual* from the Office of Strategic Services, an agency of the Joint Chiefs of Staff, to coordinate espionage activities behind enemy lines during World War II.[11] The role of art is rarely to deliver practical instruction. Art informs the imagination; it allows us to see beyond the limited possibilities afforded to us. Living under authoritarianism feels like a cage. Historical stories of resistance can inform our sense of agency in the contemporary moment. Small acts of resistance can matter.

19

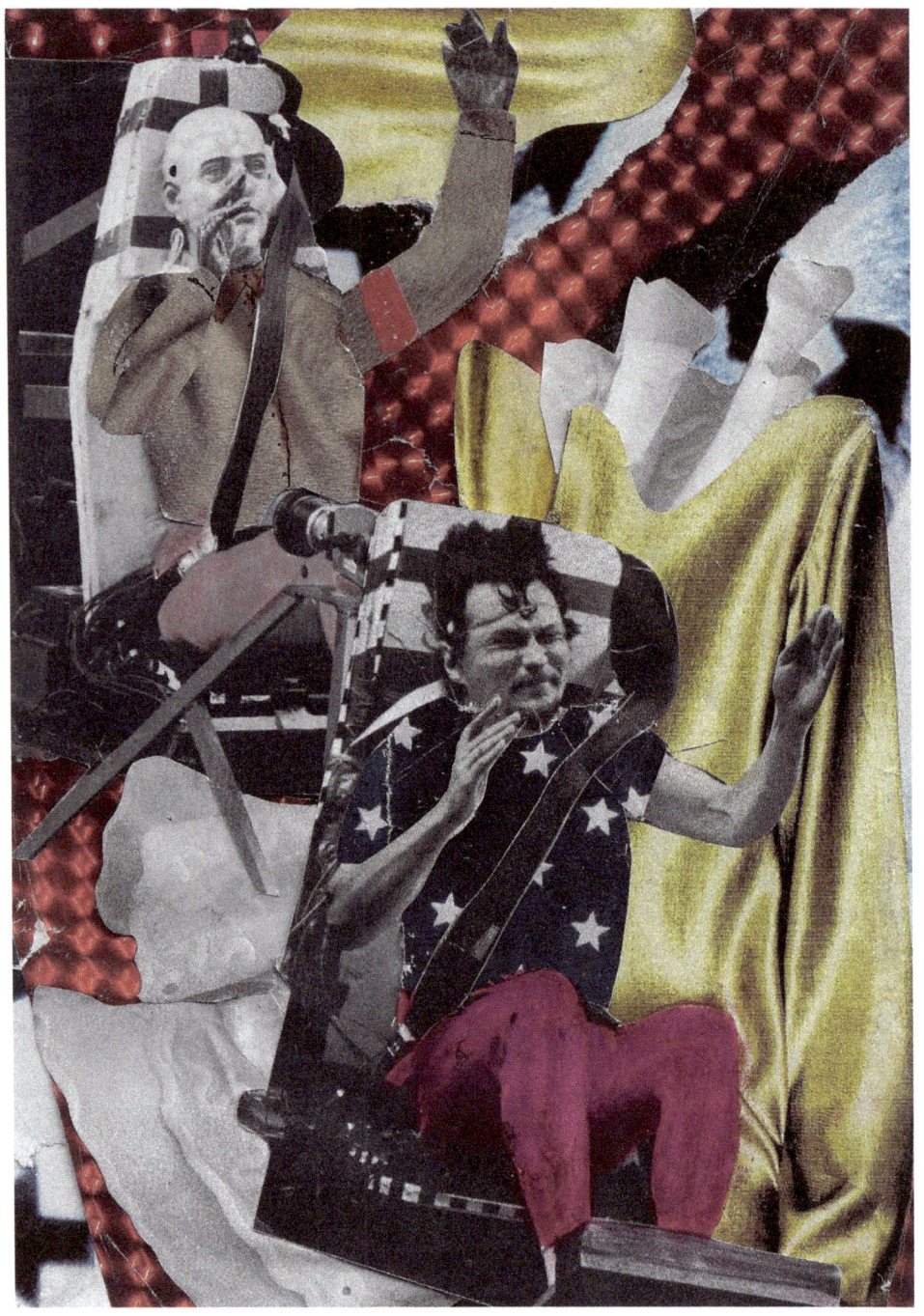

Dummies by Heather Wright

The artist wrote, "The crash test dummy, in a vintage Nazi uniform, represents prior fascist regimes that have tried and failed to take over the world. The true dummy is the democracy that has seen abysmal failures and damage but still gives it a go. The shapes and textures surrounding the figures suggest motion and chaos such as a roller coaster ride which is how the world feels when powers collide."

Taking a nod from Toni Cade Bambara's imperative to "make revolution irresistible," the collages, Wishik's *Build the Resistance*, Myhre's *Everything Old Is New Again*, and Petchers' *Power to the People*, invoke images of protest. These images normalize and celebrate protest when it is needed the most.

Our final gathering to review the collage art took place on 26 April 2025, the day after Trump's first one hundred days in office. We realized every one of the sixteen points on Mycielski's Authoritarian Checklist had occurred: A campaign of fear and false populism; the purge of institutions; cronyism; disparagement and curtailing of the press; lies to the people; false accusations of treason; illegal consequences to assembly and expression; efforts to bypass the Constitution; limits on minority and women's rights; destruction of the economy; putting the fix on the electoral system; and alienating international allies. It's as if Mycielski's warning had become a playbook.

Heather Wishik commented, "I've been thinking about the disappearing of people that's going on now and grounding that in Pinochet's…and in Putin's disappearing of people to say this is a global phenomenon. The United States has been privileged not to suffer it until now, but now we're in with the rest of them."

Yet hope is not lost. In April 2025, Bright Line Watch, a group of academics, released a survey of 760 political scientists which found, "Overall ratings of American democracy dropped significantly among every group surveyed—academic experts, the public overall, and Republican and Democratic members of the public."[12] The President's approval rating at one hundred days was an eighty-year low. People are not stupid. They understand what is happening. The challenge is, to quote the Star Wars series *Andor*, "The pace of repression outstrips our ability to understand it." Nemick, the idealistic freedom fighter, goes on to say, "And that is the real trick of the Imperial thought machine. It's easier to hide behind forty atrocities than a single incident."[13] The bombardment of news, the constant invitation to outrage, and whatever nonsensical social media posts demand our attention are a distraction from very real atrocities such as the arresting and prosecution of members of the legislature and judiciary; the horrific campaign of ICE; the gutting of government programs that safeguard the health and wellbeing of people; and what comes next.

Art is a curious antidote. Art forces us to slow down, to pause. Art invites us to learn new things, to remember old histories, to imagine different futures. In "Art and Rebellion: The Struggle for Freedom and Autonomy at the Ljubljana 2020/2021 Protests," Petja Grafenauer and Daša Tepina wrote, "When art becomes confrontational, it fights for its autonomy and its production can achieve an aesthetic revolutionary potential. So when it demands the impossible, it fights for its space and position and becomes life itself, it becomes avant-garde. We could therefore say that the politics of aesthetics has a way of producing its own politics, proposing to re-arrange politics, re-configure art as a political issue or assert itself as true politics."[14] Art is not a magical panacea for the rise of authoritarianism. Picasso's *Guernica* did not end all wars. Heartfield's collages did not bring down the Nazi regime. Authoritarianism ends because the people demand it. Gorbachev didn't

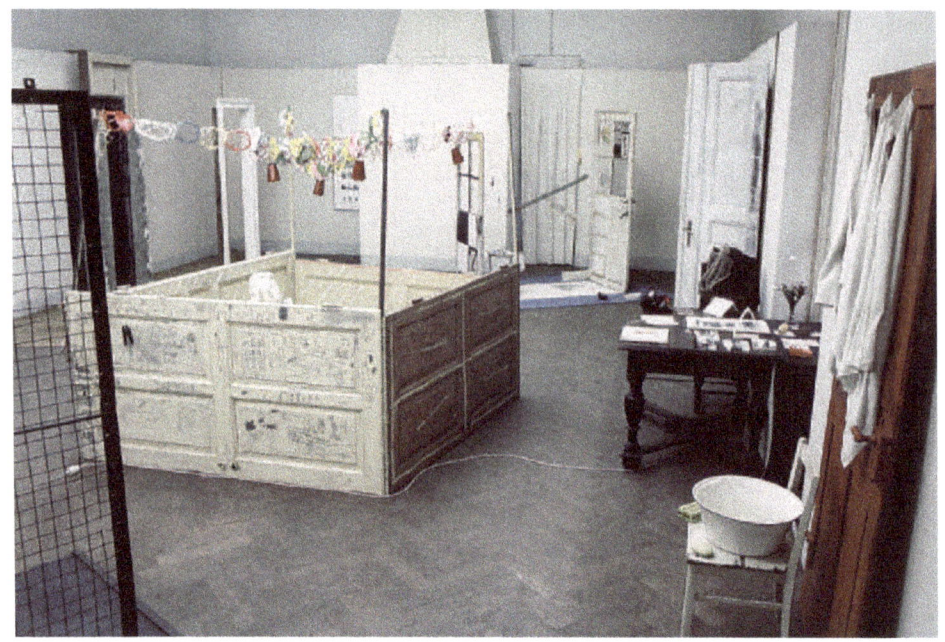

"Türenausstellung" at Leonhardi Museum Dresden (installation view)
1979. © and courtesy of Karla Woisnitza and Volker Henze.

tear down the Wall, the people of Berlin did. On 9 November 1989, civil unrest pressured the East German government to loosen travel regulations and then the people physically, brick by brick, took the wall apart. Before the people could to get to that place where they could confront authoritarianism, artists were engaged in a multigenerational campaign of resistance. April A. Eisman wrote about the history of East German art:

"It was first with the increasing hostilities of the Cold War period that modern art's role in the East began to be questioned. In October 1948, in the midst of the Berlin Blockade and less than a year before Germany was officially divided into two countries, two articles in *bildende kunst*—East(ern) Germany's professional art journal—marked the first phase of the 'formalism debates'. These articles took opposite stances on the role that art should play in society. In 'Art and Politics' (Kunst und Politik), Karl Hofer called for artistic freedom, arguing that it is up to the artist to decide on style and content, including whether or not to be political. In 'Politics and Art' (Politik und Kunst), Oskar Nerlinger argued that no art could be free from politics, even that which claimed to be, and therefore all art, as a public medium, should be accessible to the people. The latter view won out with political leaders; in their view, a realist style was a prerequisite for fulfilling this purpose."

Authoritarians rightfully see art and free expression as a threat to power. As such, they act to control what is presented, such as Trump's February 2025 removal of Kennedy Center board members appointed by his predecessor and the installation of himself as the chairman of the Board and the subsequent canceling of performances in March 2025. Authoritarians also seek to undermine existing cultural networks such as the dismantling of The Institute of Museum and Library Services through Executive Order issued on 14 March

2025 and moves to defund the National Endowment for the Arts.[15] The rise of authoritarianism is a campaign for the hearts and minds of the people. Art fundamentally threatens that campaign.

Eisman continued, "It was in this era, in August 1961, that construction began on the Berlin Wall...The result was a multi-year period of confrontation between visual artists and politicians over who had the right to determine artistic policy in East Germany. Such confrontations were not new, as evidenced by the Formalism Debate. What was new was the confidence artists exhibited in claiming the right, as part of the intellectual elite, to determine artistic policy."[16] Artists persisted. For example, in 1979 on the occasion of the 30th anniversary of the creation of East Germany, Michael Freudenberg working collaboratively in a group of eight artists installed "Türenausstellung" ("Exhibition of Doors") at the Leonhardi Museum in Dresden. An example of collage installation, the artists rejected everything that was officially sanctioned as acceptable art. "In this exhibition, each artist created their own 'door' constructions by salvaging and repurposing objects from demolished houses and junk yards," wrote Iman Salty. "The overwhelming presence of doors throughout the exhibition, each door another reflection of the other, expresses a feeling of liminality. Moving through the exhibition space, one finds themselves repeatedly confronting an ambiguous threshold. In this way, the door is a powerful symbol because it performs the lived experience of non-official artists in the GDR."[17] German artist A. R. Penck claimed it represented "the beginning of victory over false consciousness (falsches Bewußtsein)!".[18]

Art in the age of rising authoritarianism is a campaign against the false consciousness authoritarians wish to subject us to. Artists engaged in this culture work are motivated to hold space for democracy but making this art is also part of the artists own survival strategy. After our final meeting, I invited the artists to share their motivations and what they wanted viewers of the artwork and readers of this book to know. Baldacci wanted to call attention to the value of collaboration. She wrote, "I hope you see how this work was made in community even though we are not physically together. I hope our work motivates you to speak out and use art as a form of resistance." Myhre wrote, "The residency spanned the first month of the ruling regime and making political collage during that time gave me both a clarity of purpose and time working with my hands that helped turn down the volume on my fear. And I took so much solace and inspiration from what my fellow artists were wrestling with and making. My hope is that the viewer can find similar courage and wrestling and inspiration in these works to face what is happening unflinchingly and respond with love and action." Petchers wrote, "There is a helpless feeling watching one's country devolve into a dystopian version of itself. I felt trapped, afraid and in many ways alone, like a child without a parent. I wanted to do something. Working on this art project made me feel less alone and proud that I was doing my small part contributing to a greater resistance movement."

Wishick echoed this theme. "Creating at the intersection of politics and collage in community with others on Inauguration Day 2025 was for me a gasp for oxygen, for distraction, for a means of resistance. Two weeks later, our visit with Mycielski, a survivor of authoritarianism who helped his country vote them out after eight years, was the sustenance I needed to keep creating with a global view. The text has offered me guidance about what I can do, affirmation of what I am already doing, pitfalls that feel familiar and the motivation to shift away from them. Notice how the collages, in all their detailed storytelling, are in conversations with each other and the text. Let the images pull you in, inspire memory, reflection and, hopefully, the energy to mobilize with others."

Wright was motivated by a concern for how authoritarianism will disconnect us from generational knowledge. She wrote, "Perhaps you listened to parents, grandparents, and teachers speak about the struggles and battles of yesteryear. Perhaps you also saw your neighbors tout their patriotism and service in parades and print. I had all those things, and now what do my grown daughters have? They have fading contact with the people who fought those fights. They are asking me how to deal with the battle at hand, and how to prepare for the threats now in our faces. This project was a way to begin doing something, to uphold my family's tradition of getting hands dirty when the call comes. I want my children to see that they cannot glaze over, and must continue to protect what was fought for and given to them. Lest we Forget."

The rise of authoritarianism, the fall of democracies, the erasure of freedoms takes place in a fog. It's like being in a pitch black room when you can only see or touch small pieces of the animal in the room with you. A patch of rough skin here, a mass of something there, a tubular foreign object tapping you on your shoulder, some quiet grunts, an off smell. By the time you realize it's an elephant, it's too late to do anything but to try and get out of the room (and you hope it's not blocking the door) or try to keep from being trampled. If you are predisposed to believe that an elephant can't exist in a room or that the elephant won't hurt you or that the elephant has your interests in mind, then you may never quite see it… until you are forced to reckon with it. At any given moment, some of us are on the wrong side of history but we don't know it. My hope is that this book and these artworks will help us understand the elephant in the room, and perhaps more importantly, remind us that we are not alone with the elephant.

—Ric Kasini Kadour

SOURCES

1 Foucault, Michel. (2003). *"Society must be defended": Lectures at the Collège de France, 1975-1976*. (David Macey, Trans.). Picador.

2 Open Dialogue Foundation. (2025). *Team: Martin Mycielski*. en.odfoundation.eu.

3 Mycielski, Martin. (2025, January 26). Presentation to Politics in Collage Residency 2025, Session 2 [Zoom recording].

4 Mycielski, Martin. (2018, March 26). *The authoritarian regime survival guide*. Verfassungsblog. www.verfassungsblog.de.

5 Martin Mycielski (personal communication, November 7, 2024). Only ten minutes elapsed between Kadour's initial email and Mycielski's response.

6 Kadour, Ric Kasini. (2025, January 19). Presentation to Politics in Collage Residency 2025, Session 1 [Zoom recording].

7 *Our history* (n.d.). Freedom House www.freedomhouse.org.

8 Repucci, Sarah & Slipowitz, Amy. (2022). "The global expansion of authoritarian rule" in *Freedom in the World 2022*. Freedom House.

9 Library of Congress. (n.d.). *1942: Bracero program*. guides.loc.gov.

10 The Federal Bureau of Investigation. (n.d.). *COINTELPRO. FBI Records: The Vault*. vault.fbi.gov.

11 Strategic Services (Provisional). (1944). *Simple sabotage field manual*. Office of Strategic Services.

12 Bright Line Watch. (2025). *Threats to democracy and academic freedom after Trump's second first 100 days*. www.brightlinewatch.org.

13 *Andor*, Season 1, Episode 5.

14 Grafenauer, Petja & Tepina, Daša. (2022). Art and rebellion: The struggle for freedom and autonomy at Ljubljana 2020/2021 protests. *Third Text, 36*(5), 409-428.

15 Exec. Order No. 14,238, 90 FR 13043 (2025). *Continuing the reduction of the federal bureaucracy*. www.federalregister.gov.

16 Eisman, April A. (2011). East German art and cultural politics. *ART/WORK Six Shorts* [text accompanying the DVD]. DEFA Film Library.

17 Salty, Iman. (2023). Doorway to dissidence: The 1979 doors exhibition in the GDR. *react/review: a responsive journal for art & architecture 3*, 96-102.

18 Weissbach, Angelika. (2014). "Das ist der Anfang der Überwindung des falschen Bewusstseins!": Die Türen-Ausstellung im Leonhardi-Museum in Dresden. *OwnReality* (5).

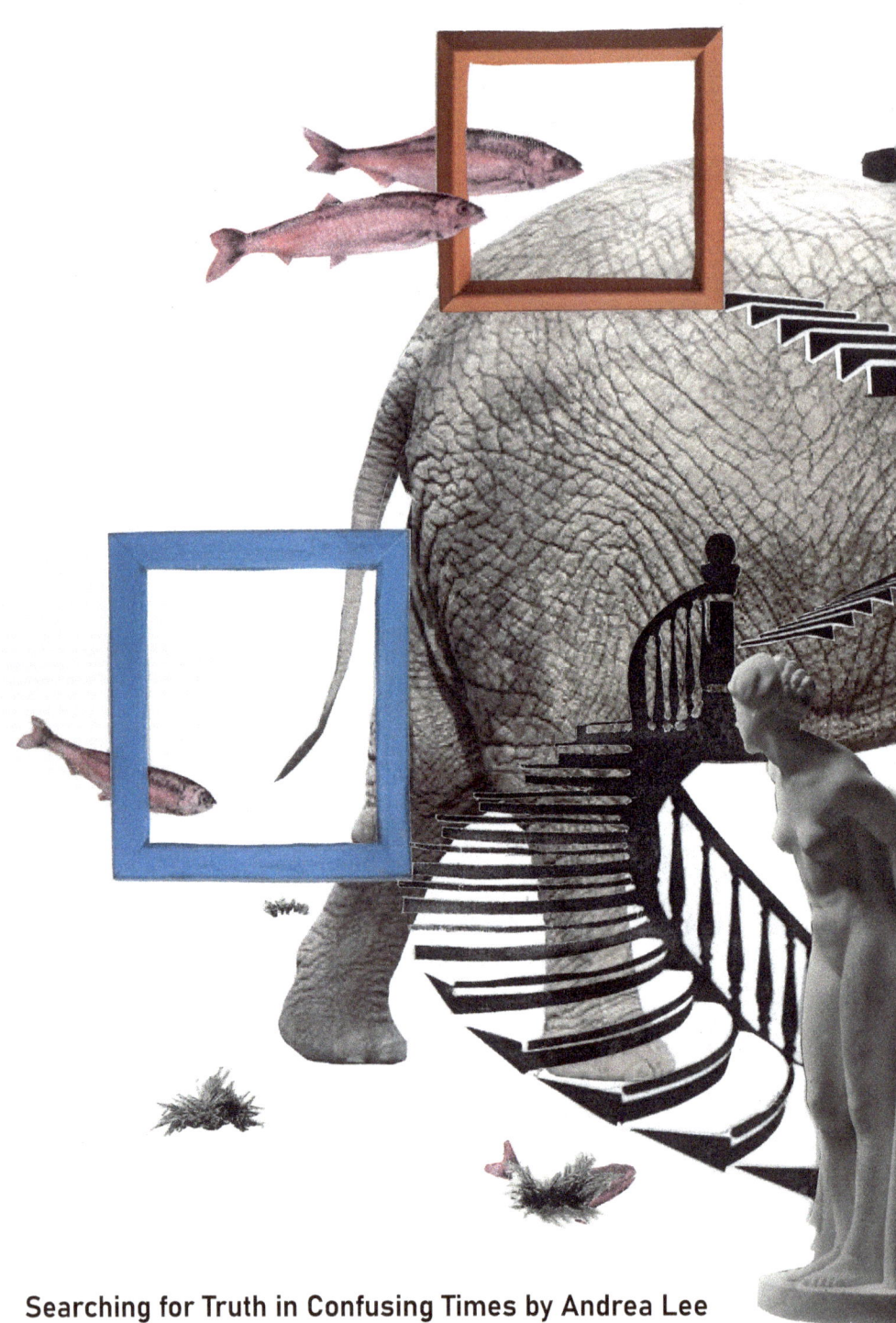

Searching for Truth in Confusing Times by Andrea Lee

Referencing a Sufi fable of blind men touching an elephant, Lee wrote, "The frames denote limited points of view, the scattered red herring distractions, and the woman stands frozen by her search for the heart of the matter. Red and blue add a layer of meaning for US viewers for whom the colours convey political affiliation, and the small red and blue frame suggests the possibility of a truth that can be agreed upon."

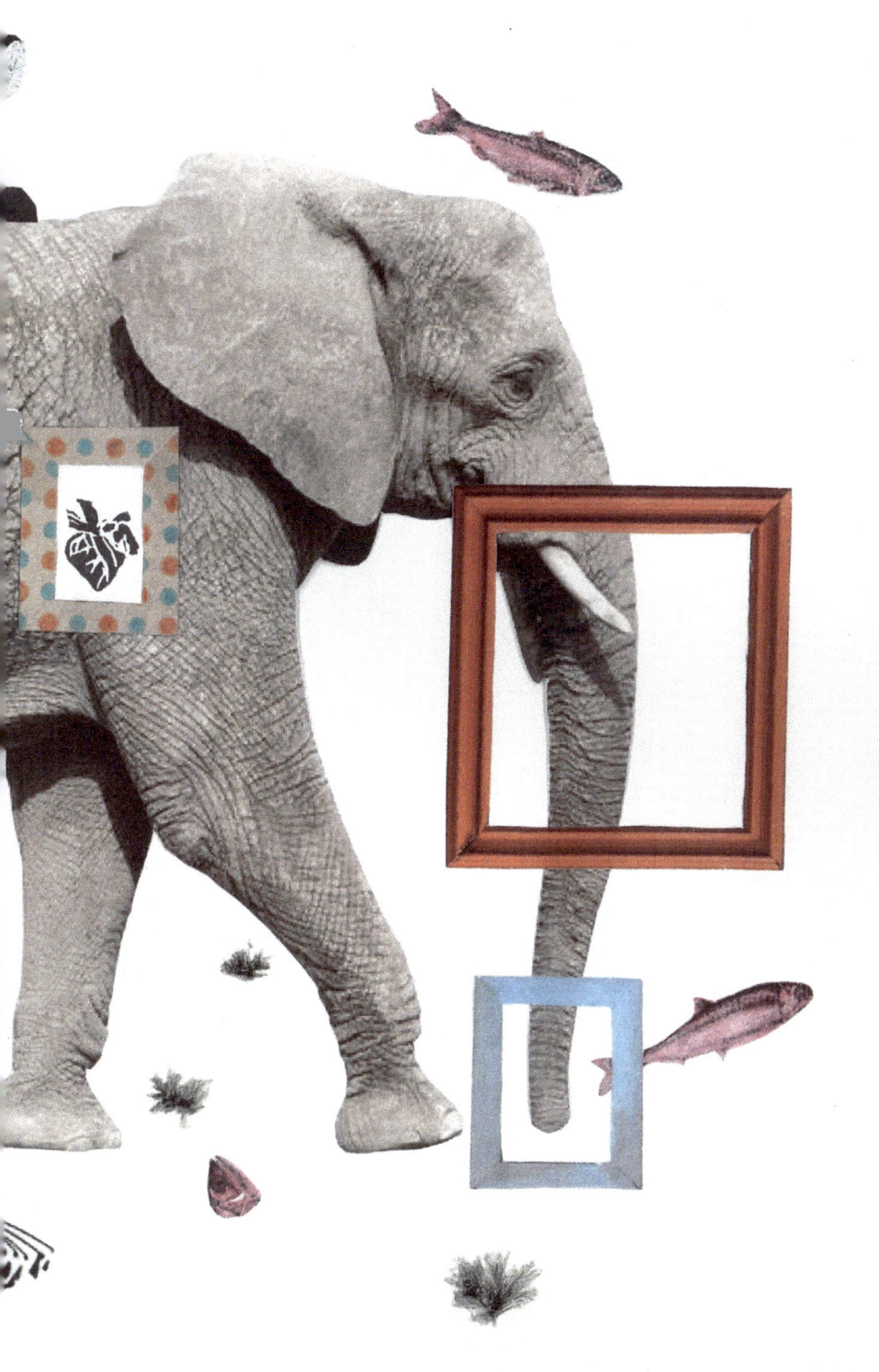

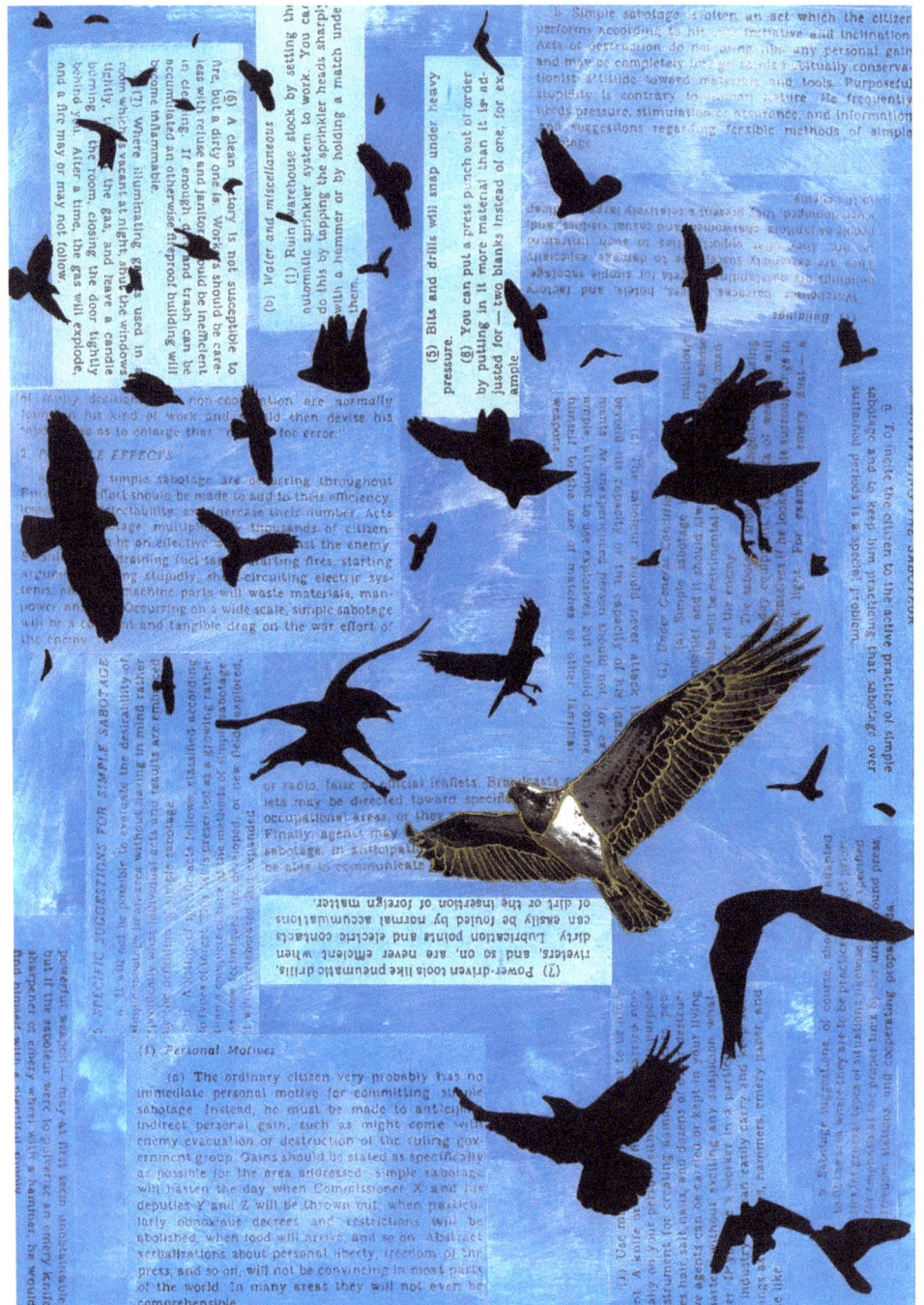

Specific Suggestions for Simple Sabotage by Jennifer R Myhre

A murder of crows flies against a blue sky made of fragments from the U.S. Central Intelligence Agency's 1944 declassified *Simple Sabotage Manual*. The pamphlet instructs agents on how to recruit and train citizen-saboteurs in simple methods to resist authoritarian regimes. "The weapons of the citizen-saboteur are salt, nails, candles, pebbles, thread, or any other materials he might normally be expected to possess as a householder." Myhre drew on her knowledge of birds when she chose crows as the symbol of such actors. The artist wrote, "Crows, even though they are much smaller than hawks, are usually pretty good about annoying a hawk away if they collectively squawk at it."

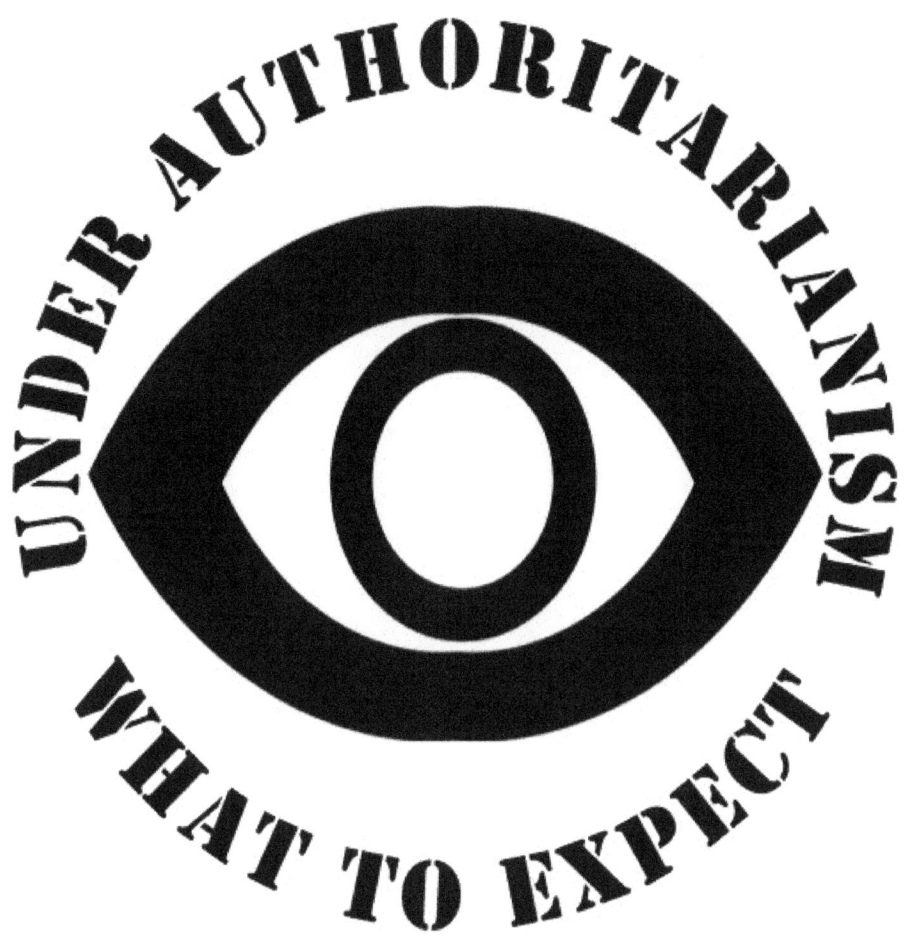

How to spot Authoritarianism in action?

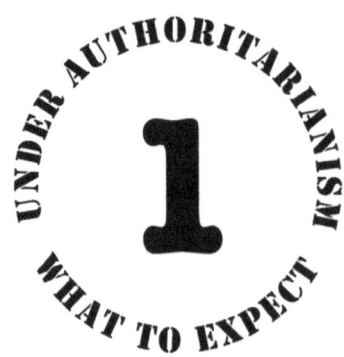

UNDER AUTHORITARIANISM — WHAT TO EXPECT — 1

They will come to power with a campaign based on fear, scaremongering and distorting the truth.

Nevertheless, their victory will be achieved through a democratic electoral process.

But beware, as this will be their argument every time you question the legitimacy of their actions.

They will claim a mandate from the People to change the system.

**Remember:
gaining power
through a democratic system does not
give them
permission to cross
legal boundaries and undermine said
democracy.**

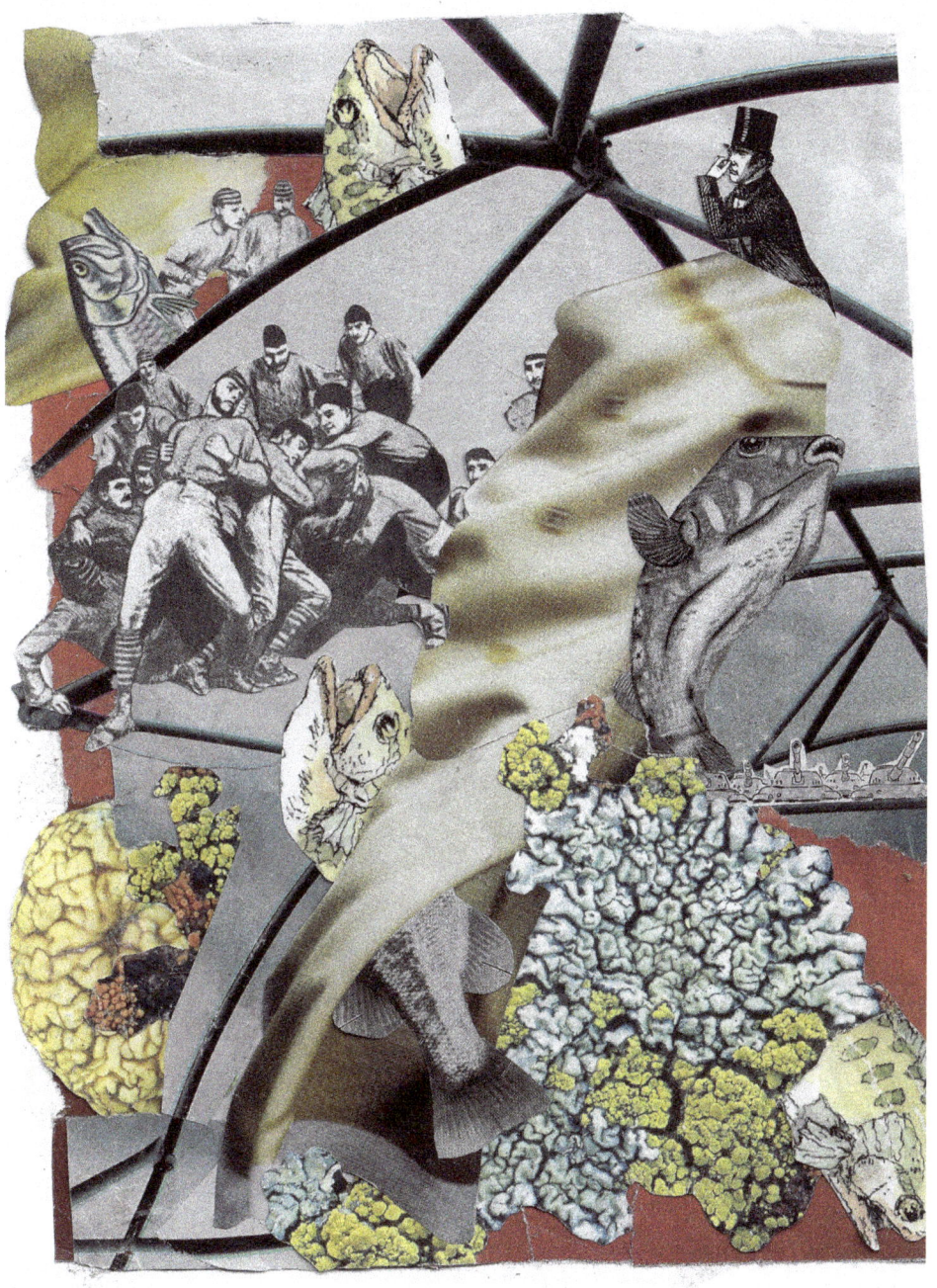

PU a Coup by Heather Wright

What does authoritarianism smell like? Wright's collage wants us to think of the "pee-ew" of dead fish. She wrote, "The textural pieces indicate decay, the fabric in the middle is beginning to bruise or rot. Citizens are divided and fighting among themselves while the elected just watch and do nothing to prevent the coup. The results of authoritarianism winning would smell worse than rotting fish."

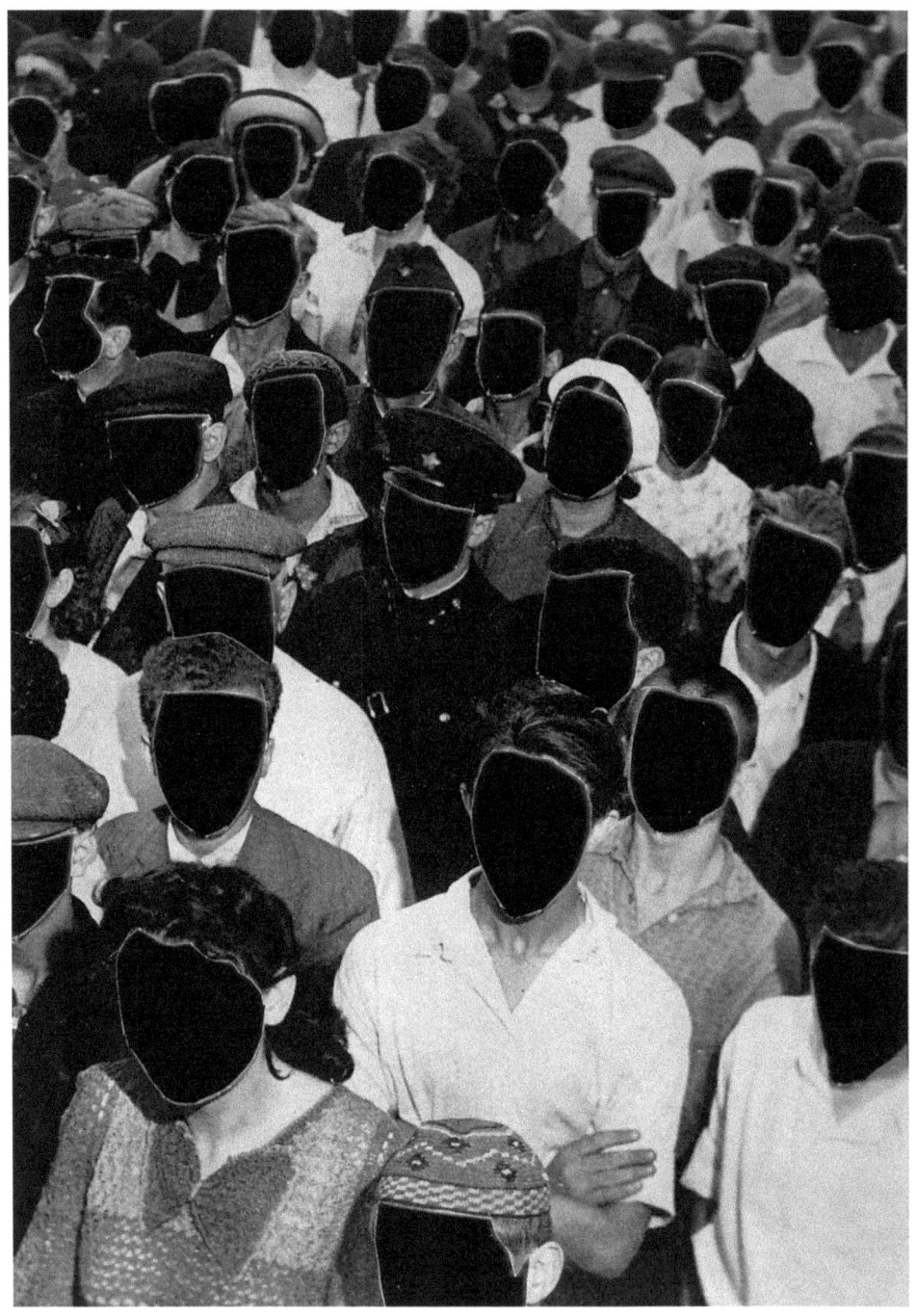

The Town Square by Lori Petchers

Using a photograph published in *LIFE* magazine, Lori Petchers collages over the face of people living in 1950s Soviet Union. The artist wrote, "The people are faceless in this collage, to remind us what it is like in a place where public assembly is not legal, people cannot show their identity or they will be arrested...Authoritarians don't allow public assembly unless it is in support of their cause. I would like the viewer to imagine what it would be like to live in such a restricted world."

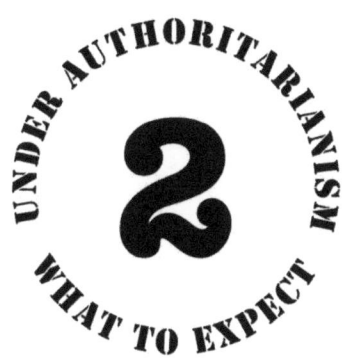

UNDER AUTHORITARIANISM — WHAT TO EXPECT

They will divide and rule. Their strength lies in unity, in one voice and one ideology, and so should yours.

They will call their supporters Patriots, the only "true Americans".

You will be labelled as traitors, enemies of the state, unpatriotic, the corrupt elite, the old regime trying to regain power.

Their supporters will be the "People", the "sovereign" who chose their leaders.

> **Don't let them divide you.**
>
> **Remember, you are one People, one Nation, with one common good.**

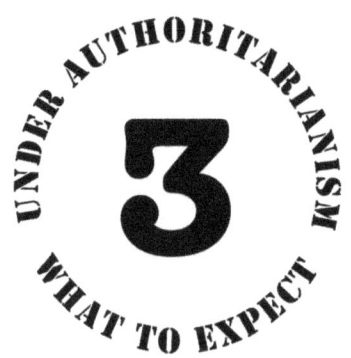

They will subjugate state media, turning them into a propaganda tube. Then, through convoluted laws and threats they will attempt to control all mainstream media and limit press freedom.

They will ban critical press from their briefings, calling them "liars", "fake news".

They will brand those media as "unpatriotic", acting against the People.

> **Fight for every media outlet, every journalist that is being banned, censored, sacked or labelled an "enemy of the state." There's no hope for freedom where there is no free press.**

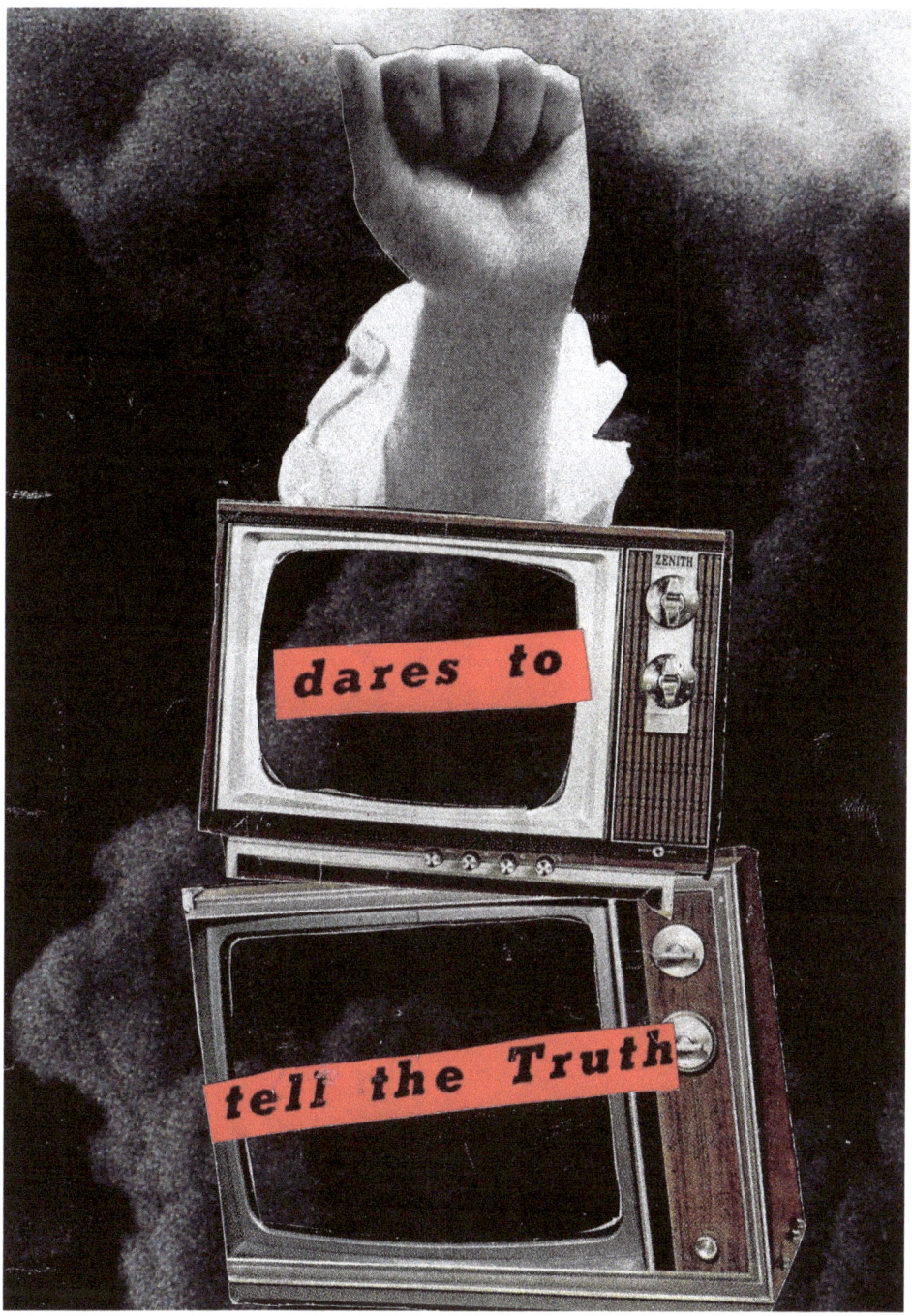

Truth and Dare by Lori Petchers

The fist in this collage is taken from a photograph of Miss Montana Kathy Huppe published in the 18 September 1970 issue of *LIFE* magazine. Huppe resigned her title after pageant officials forbade her from taking part in political activities. The red writing is from the 1940s liberal, anti-facist magazine *FRIDAY*, whose slogan is "The Magazine which dares to tell the Truth". The artist wrote, "I want the viewer to support media outlets and journalists who are being silenced or oppressed."

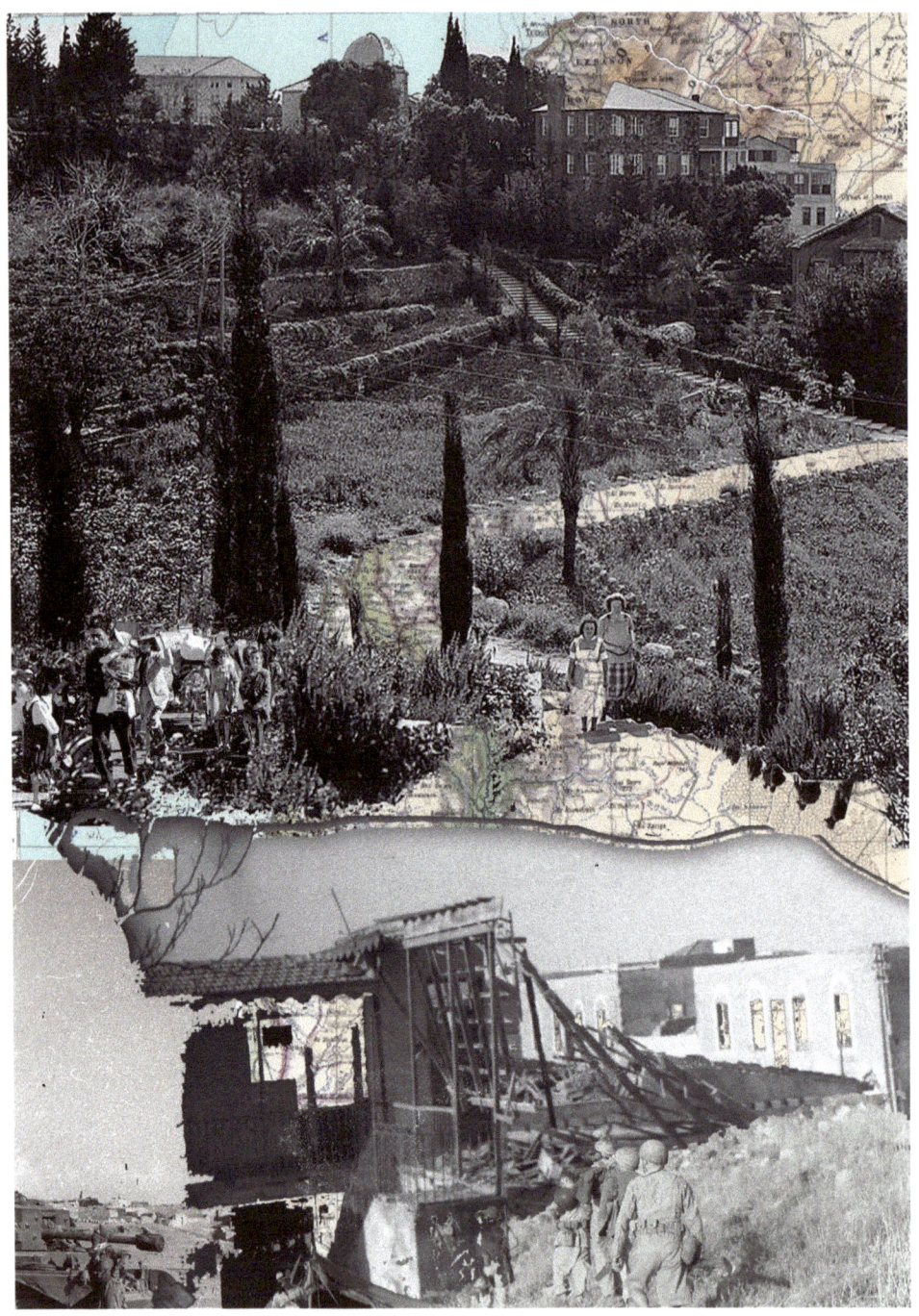

Promised Land by Olivia Baldacci

Baldacci's collage speaks to the authoritarian regime's need for a constant state of conflict and danger. She juxtaposes landscape and map images of Lebanon and Palestine with destroyed buildings. She wrote, "Forced displacement is inherently violent, relying on chaos and confusion to further harm marginalized populations. I hope the viewer considers the real life consequences, regardless of the location of this displacement. If you see one occupation as wrong, then all occupations are wrong."

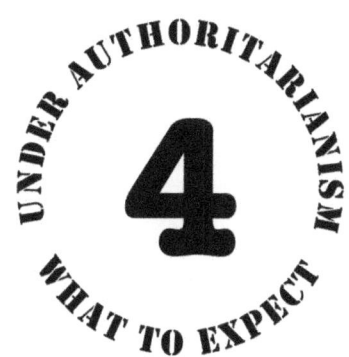

4
UNDER AUTHORITARIANISM — WHAT TO EXPECT

They will create chaos, maintain a constant sense of conflict and danger.

It will be their argument to enact new authoritarian laws, each one further limiting your freedoms and civil liberties.

They will disguise them as being for your protection, for the good of the People.

See through the chaos, the fake danger, expose it before you wake up in a totalitarian, fascist state.

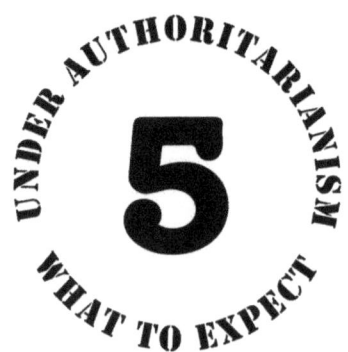

They will distort the truth, deny facts and blatantly lie.

They will try to make you forget what facts are, sedate your need to find the truth.

They will feed "post-truths" and "alternative facts", replace knowledge and logic with emotions and fiction.

Always think critically, fact-check and point out the truth, expose ignorance with facts.

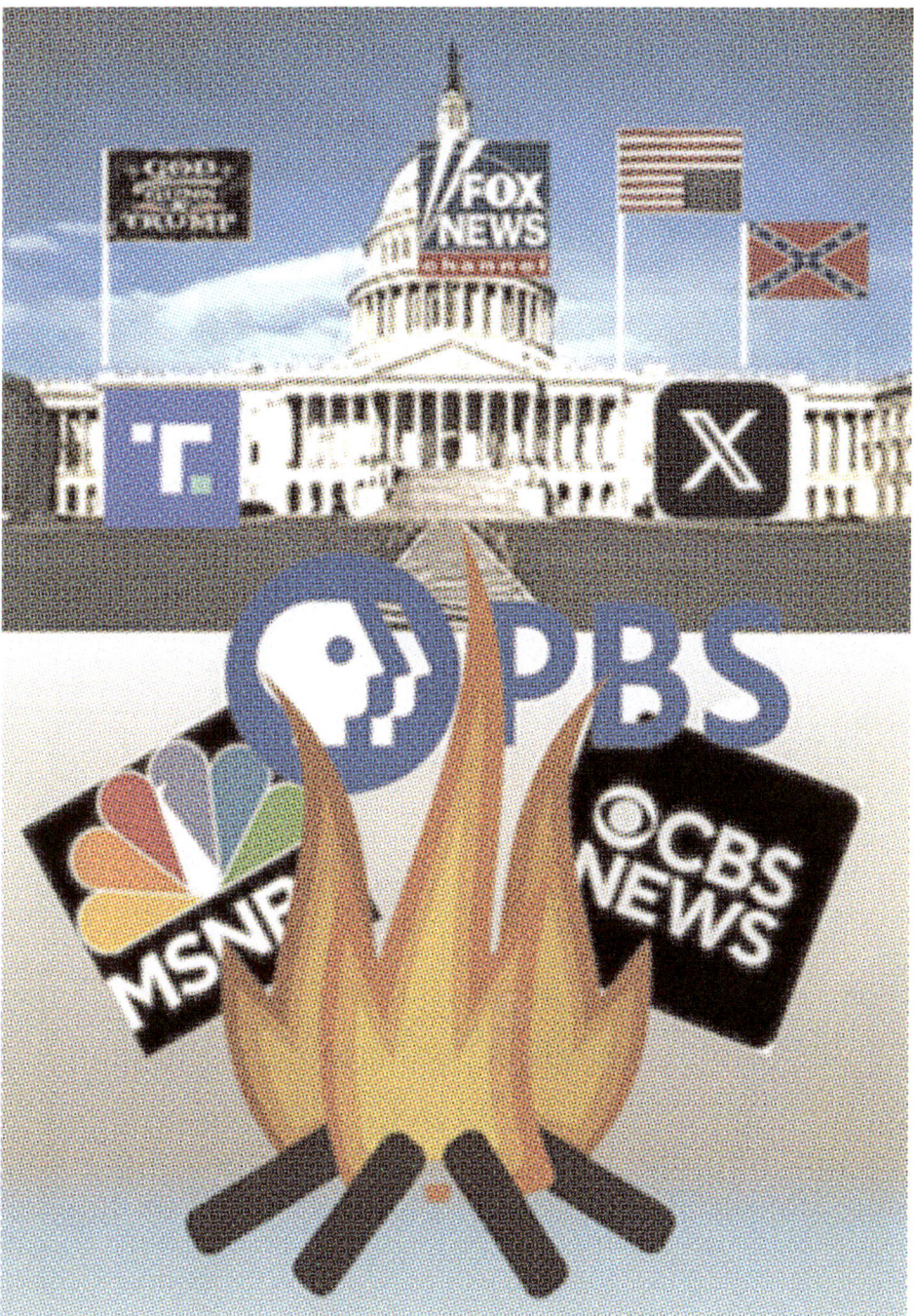

Loyalties by Suzanne Gore

A collage of digital images speaks to the chaos and complexity of a media landscape where loyalty to ideology supersedes professional standards. The artist wrote, "The bonfire is an allusion to book-burning. It speaks to both the takeover of symbols and of media, particularly raising FOX News, Truth Social and X up and trying to eliminate PBS, MSNBC, while Trump sues CBS News over a Kamala Harris interview on *60 Minutes*. The burning of these media outlets represents both an element of censorship and constitutes a severe loss of information and cultural heritage. It shows the contempt for news sources is intended to conceal and control public knowledge and opinion."

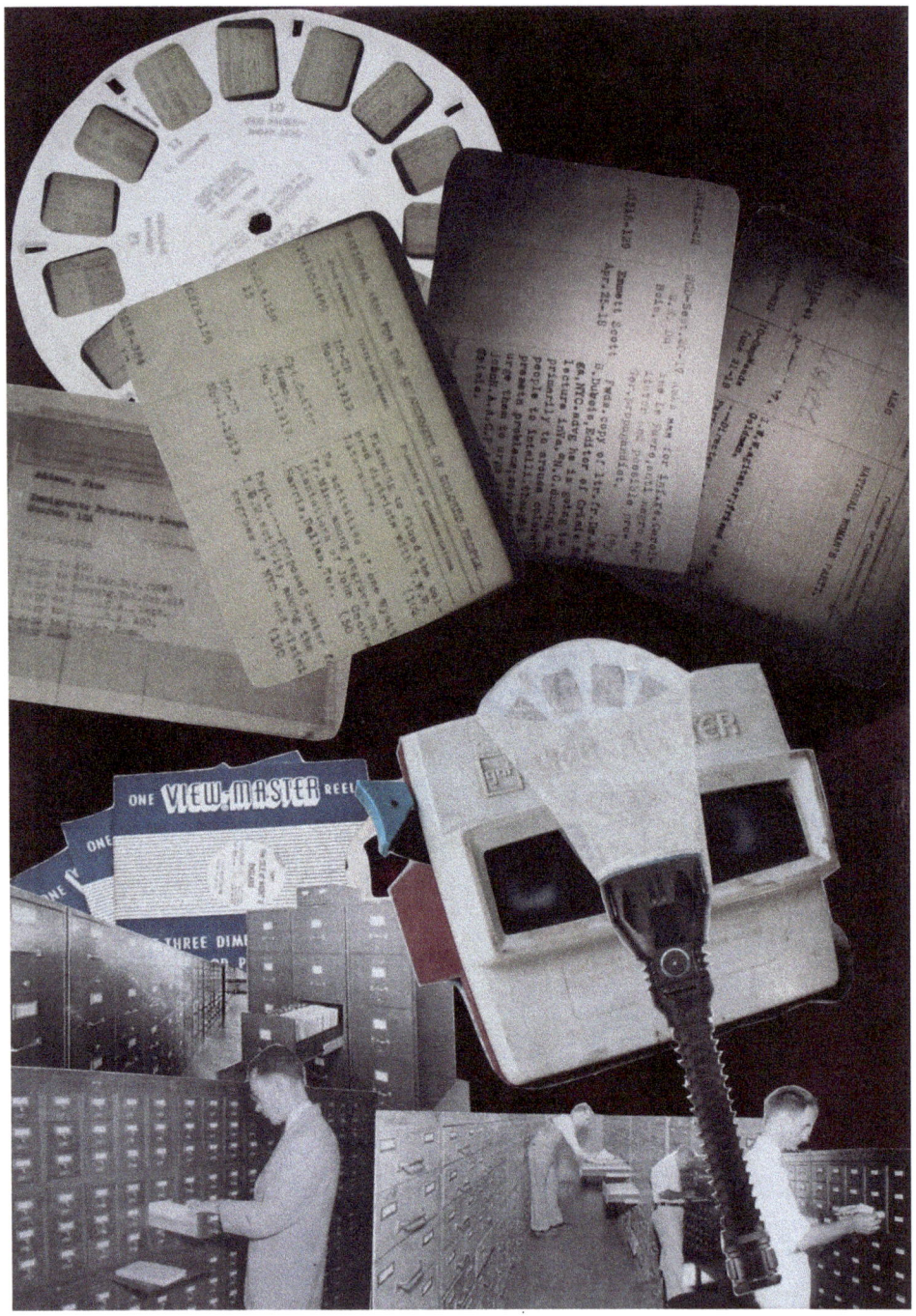

Who Is Watching the Watchers? by Jennifer R Myhre

The artist wrote, "This collage uses images from U.S. Military Intelligence files from the late 1910s and early 1920s, found in the National Archives. Military Intelligence was surveilling progressives from the labor movement, civil rights movement and women's movements in a period parallel to our own in which capitalist fascism and xenophobia was on the rise in the U.S. It points to the toxic use of nostalgia by authoritarian elites."

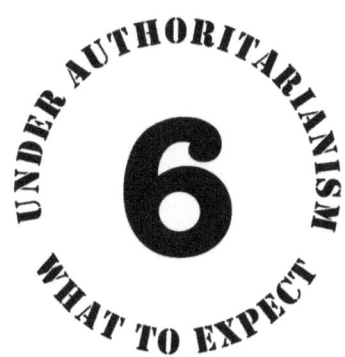

They will incite and then leak fake, superficial "scandals".

They will smear opposition with trivial accusations, blowing them out of proportion and then feeding the flame.

This is just smokescreen for the legal steps they will be taking towards totalitarianism.

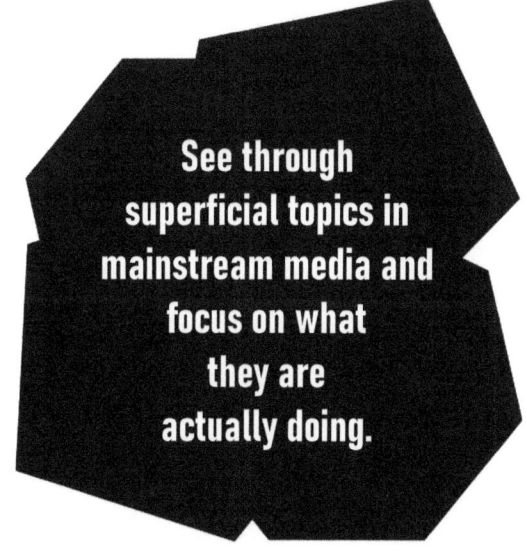

See through superficial topics in mainstream media and focus on what they are actually doing.

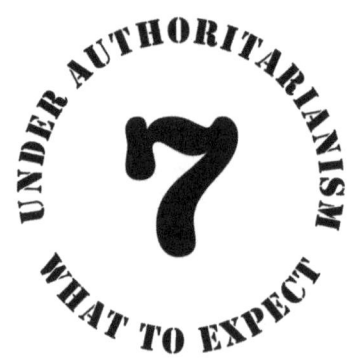

UNDER AUTHORITARIANISM: WHAT TO EXPECT — 7

They will propose shocking laws to provoke your outrage.

You will focus your efforts on fighting them, so they will seemingly back off, giving you a false sense of victory.

In the meantime they will push through less "flashy" legislation, slowly dismantling democracy.

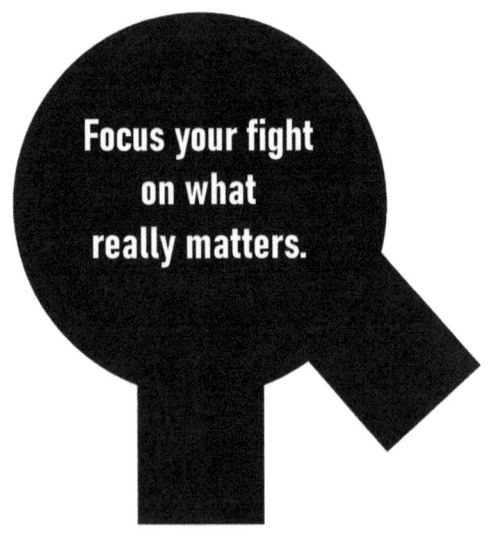

Focus your fight on what really matters.

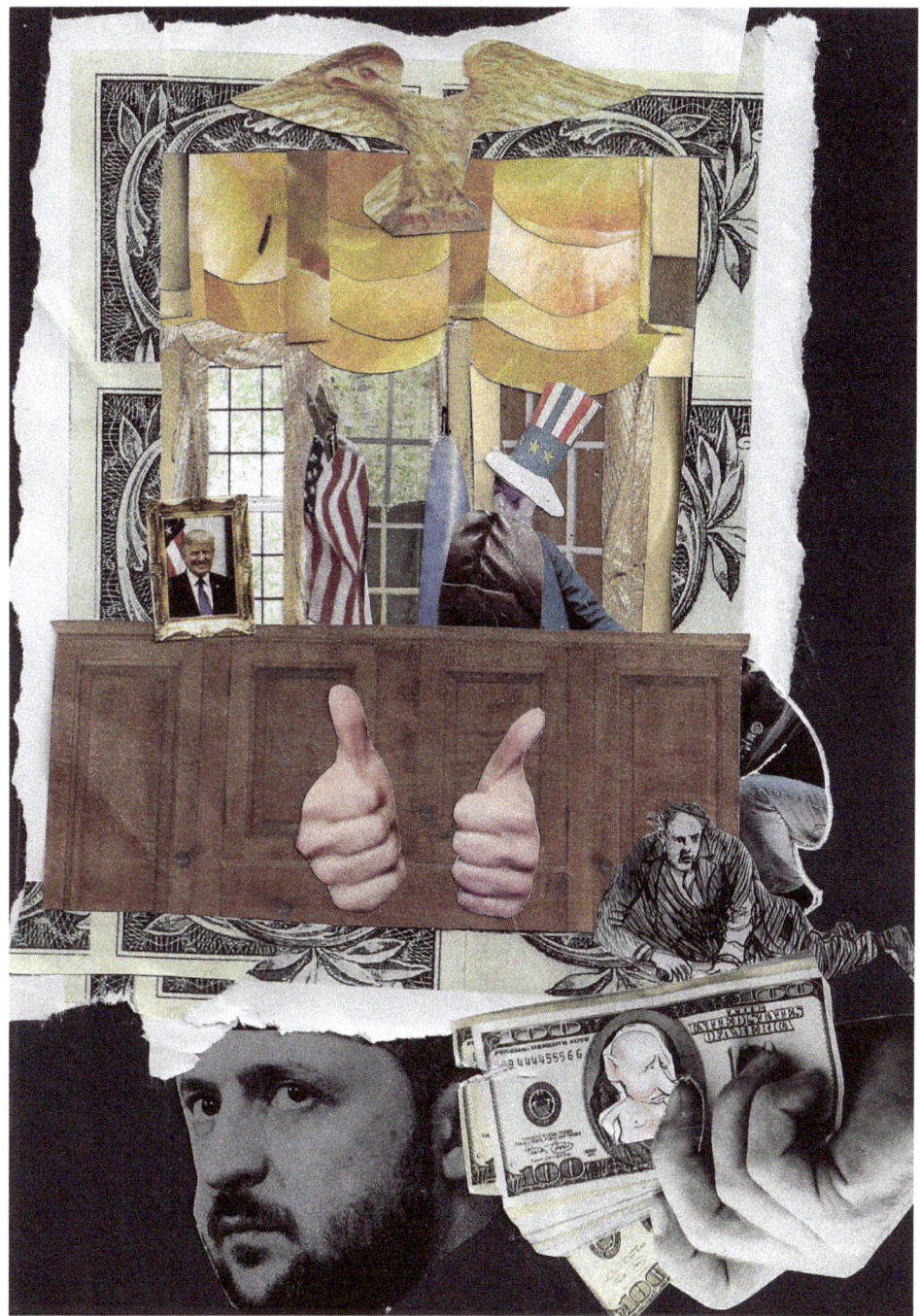

Ingrates by Heather Wright

Wright's collage is made in response to the contentious 28 February 2025 meeting between Donald Trump, JD Vance, and Volodymyr Zelenskyy in the Oval Office. The artist wrote, "The full flag of authoritarianism was flying over this country that day. Musk's thumbs up offer a flippant attitude to corruption...Uncle Sam's evil twin is having a Clinton-esque session at the desk with the People while those used and discarded lie dazed at his feet. Dirty Russian money is flaunted at the corrupt government while Ukraine is staring in defiance and disgust, but also fear, as the bad guys advance and gain cronies. Currency surrounding the scene emphasizes how little humanity matters."

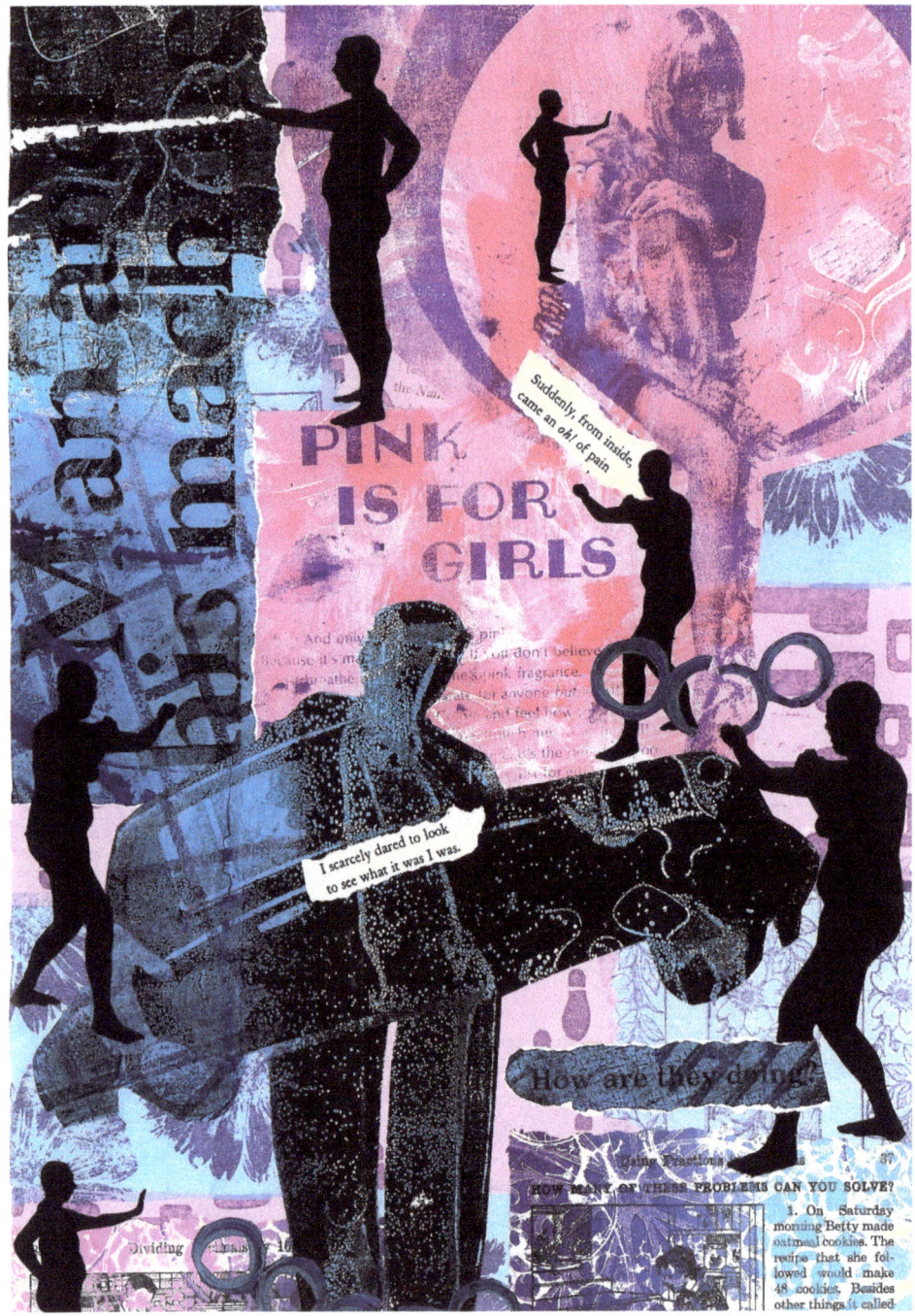

Pink Is for Girls by Jennifer R Myhre

This abstract collage is made of various cultural fragments that speak to or about women and their role in society. Myhre wrote, "Biological determinism has been a central narrative in the rise of authoritarianism in the US, paralleling Nazism and Putin's Russia. This collage asks the viewer to question gender ideologies using materials which socialize us into particular gender roles and categories, such as mass media and education."

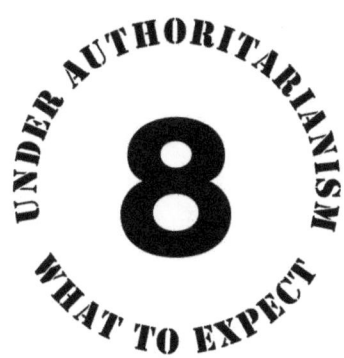

8 — UNDER AUTHORITARIANISM: WHAT TO EXPECT

When invading your liberal sensibilities they will focus on what hurts the most—women and minorities. They will act as if democracy was majority rule without respect for the minority. They will paint foreigners and immigrants as potential threats. Racial, religious, sexual and other minorities will become enemies to the order and security they are supposedly providing. They will challenge women's social status, undermine gender equality and interfere with reproductive rights. But it means they are aware of the threat women and minorities pose to their rule, so make it your strength.

> **Women and minorities have to be ready to fight the hardest —reminding the majority what true democracy is about—and you must fight together with them.**

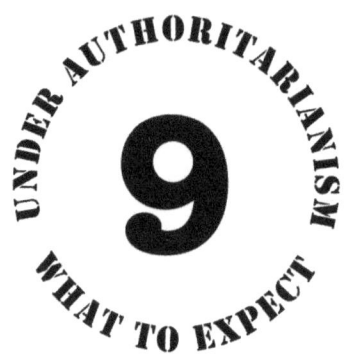

9 — UNDER AUTHORITARIANISM / WHAT TO EXPECT

They will try to take control of the judiciary.

They will assault your highest court. They need to remove the checks and balances to be able to push through unconstitutional legislation.

Controlling the judiciary they can also threat anyone that defies them with prosecution, including the press.

> **Preserve the independence of your courts at all cost, they are your safety valve, the safeguard of the rule of law and the democratic system.**

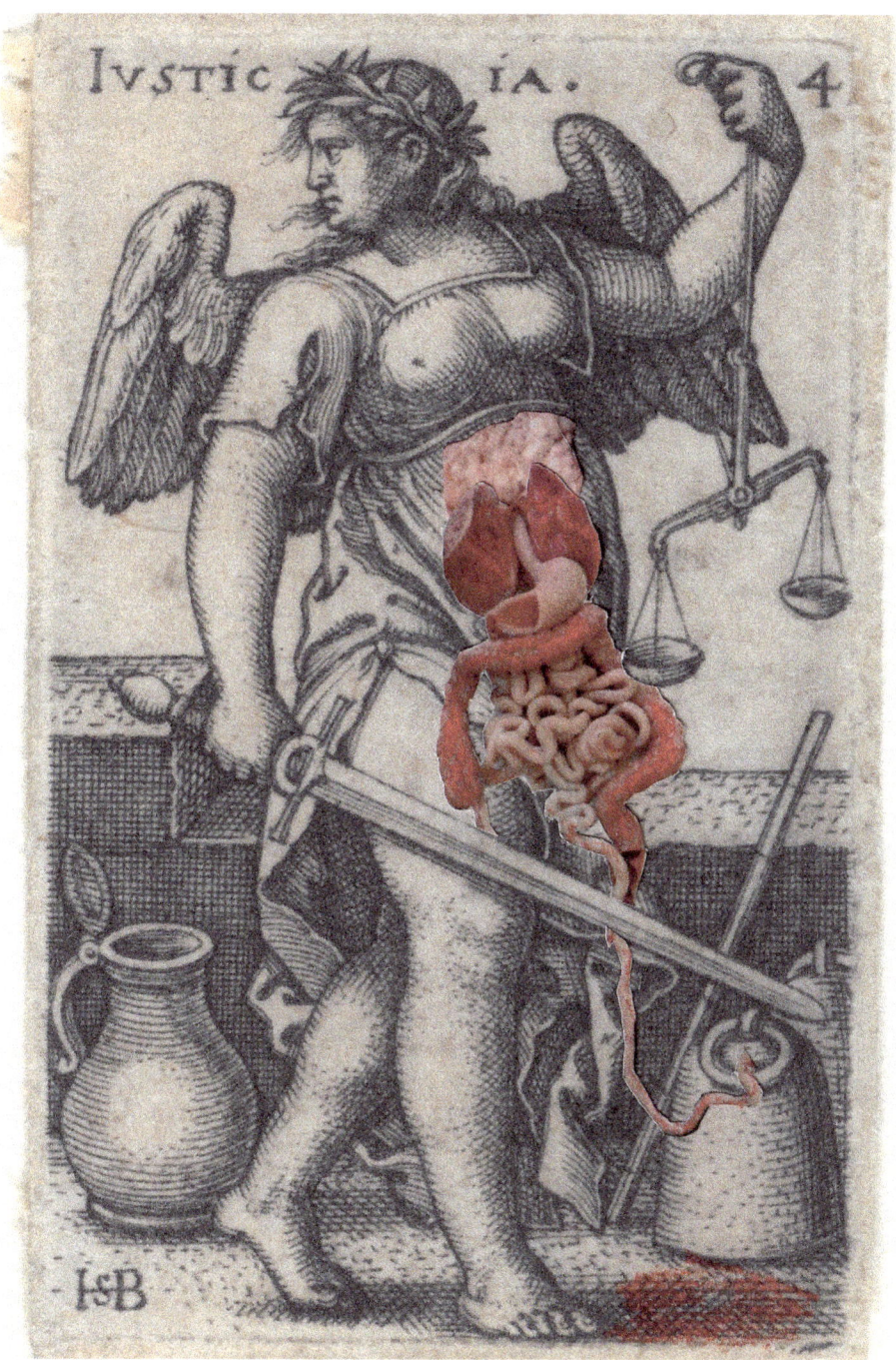

Gutting Justice by Lori Petchers

With this collage, Petchers wants to make visceral the idea that authoritarian regimes "disembowel our legal system." The central image is 16th century German printmaker Hans Sebald Beham's engraving, *Justice* from his "The Seven Virtues" series found in the digital collections of the New York Public Library. "In my art practice, I like to use the minimal amount of images to make the maximum impact." wrote the artist. "To create the guts, I combined two images which I cut and colored. I used crayon for the blood on the floor."

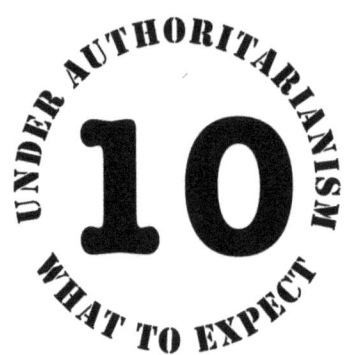

They will try to limit freedom of assembly, calling it a necessity for your security.

They will enact laws prioritizing state events and rallies, or those of a certain type or ideology.

If they can choose who can demonstrate legally, they have a legal basis to forcefully disperse or prosecute the rest.

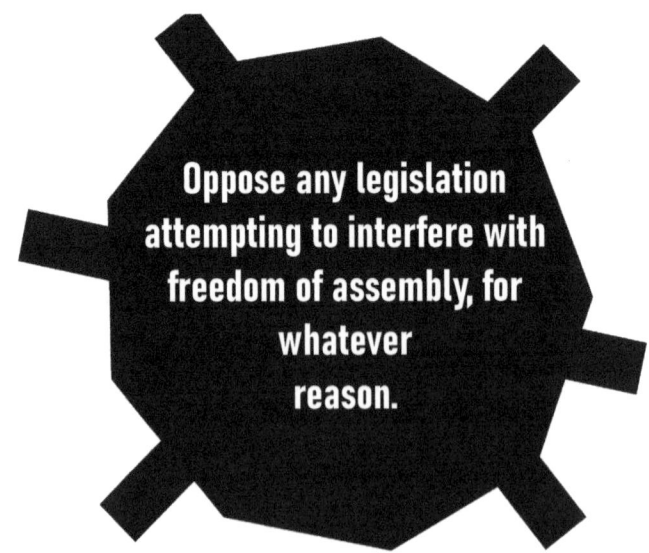

Oppose any legislation attempting to interfere with freedom of assembly, for whatever reason.

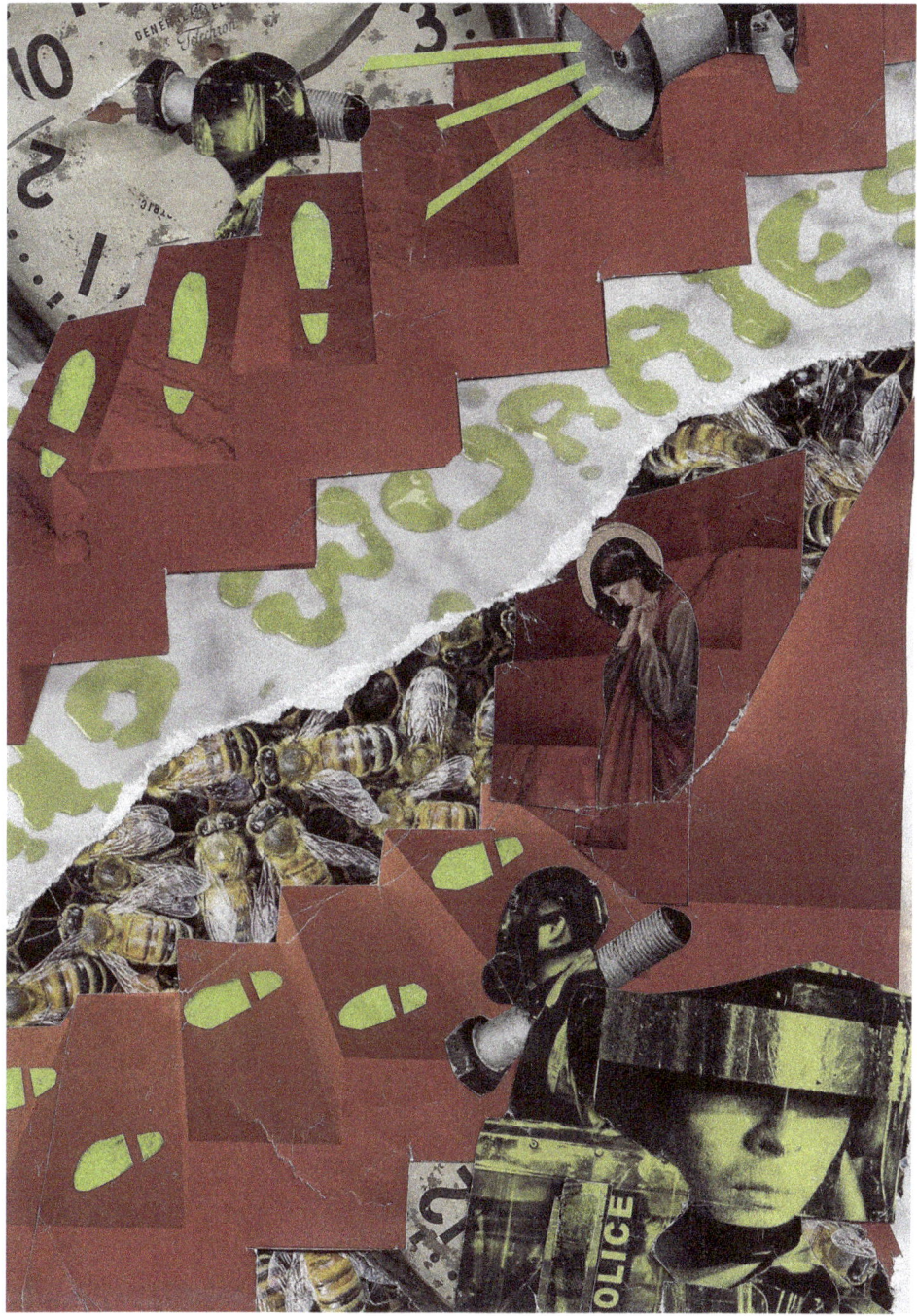

No Worries by Heather Wright

Wright's collage is a response to news reports of immigration police rounding up and imprisoning people. The artist wrote, "There are steps leading up to prosperity and down to despair. ICE is swarming the country, ejecting citizens and visitors, as others watch with apathy. This is happening in a chaotic, rapid time frame. The clocks are also dazed. The megaphone berates anyone trying to reach for something better. Those footsteps that look like exclamation points are hurried down into despair where more ICE agents await."

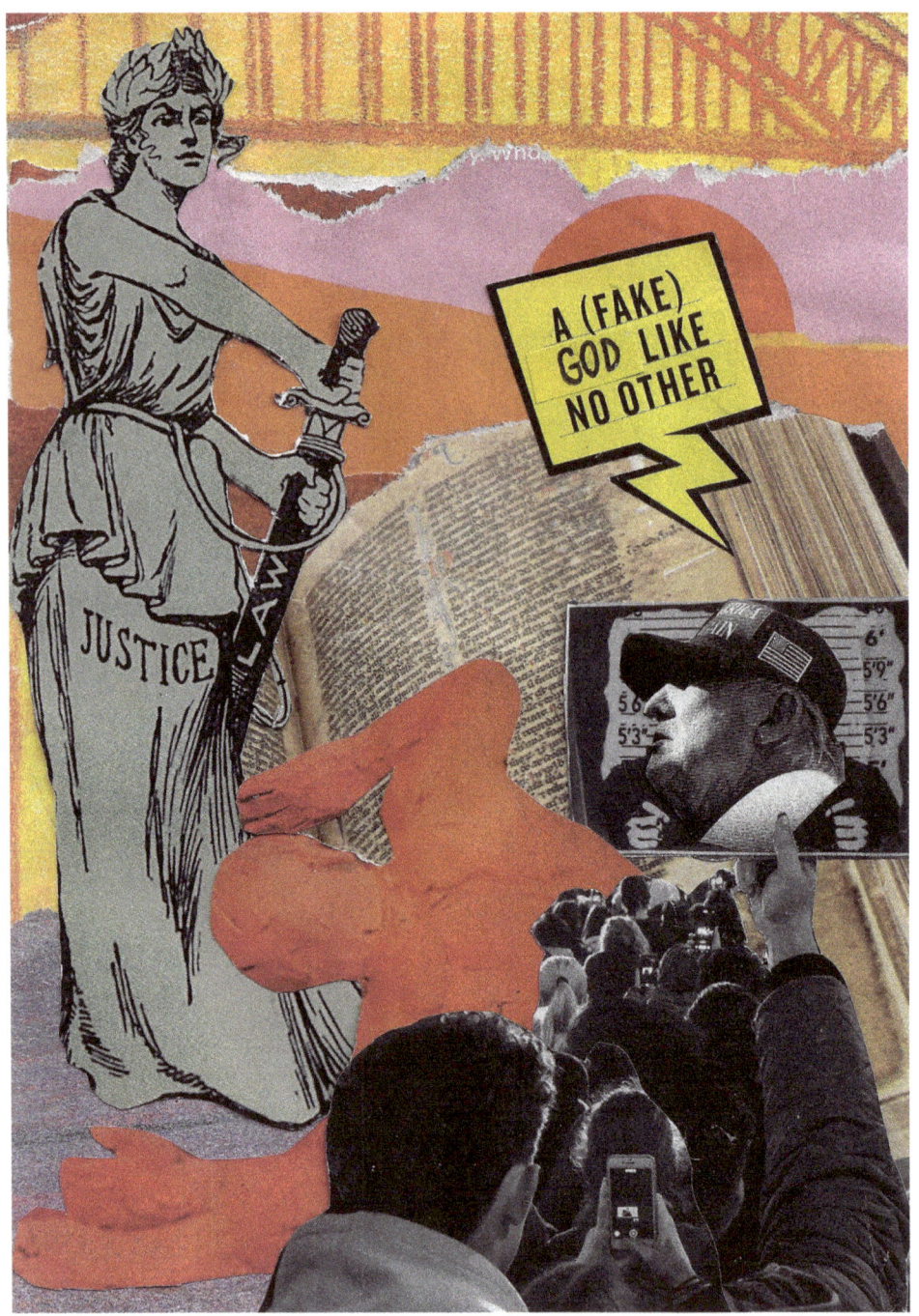

Thou Shalt Not Compromise Our Democracy by Heather Wright

In this collage, Wright casts the figure of Justice as a warrior in a morality play about religion and democracy. The artist wrote, "The rule of law in a democracy is sacred. In this piece, Justice is asserting that rule of law against the Threat that has molded itself into the image of the fake god. The image of Trump is shown against a police lineup wall, the crowd in denial of his guilt. The bible is depicted as large and formidable but still behind Justice and The Law."

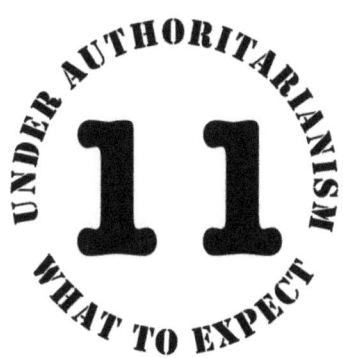

11 — UNDER AUTHORITARIANISM: WHAT TO EXPECT

They will distort the language, coin new terms and labels, repeat shocking phrases until you accept them as normal and subconsciously associate them with whom they like.

A "thief", "liar" or "traitor" will automatically mean the opposition, while a "patriot" or a "true American" will mean their follower.

Their slogans will have double meaning, giving strength to their supporters and instilling angst in their opponents.

> **Fight changes in language in the public sphere, remind and preserve the true meaning of words.**

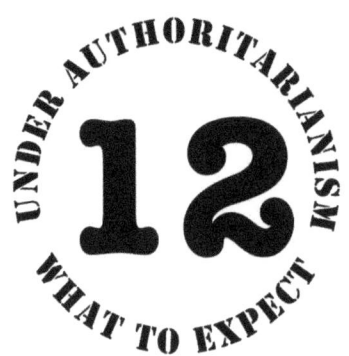

They will take over your national symbols, associate them with their regime, remake them into attributes of their power.

They want you to forget that your flag, your anthem and your symbols belong to you, the People, to everyone equally.

Don't let them be hijacked.

Use and expose them in your fight as much as they do.

> **Show your national symbols with pride, let them give you strength, not associate you with the tyranny they brought onto your country.**

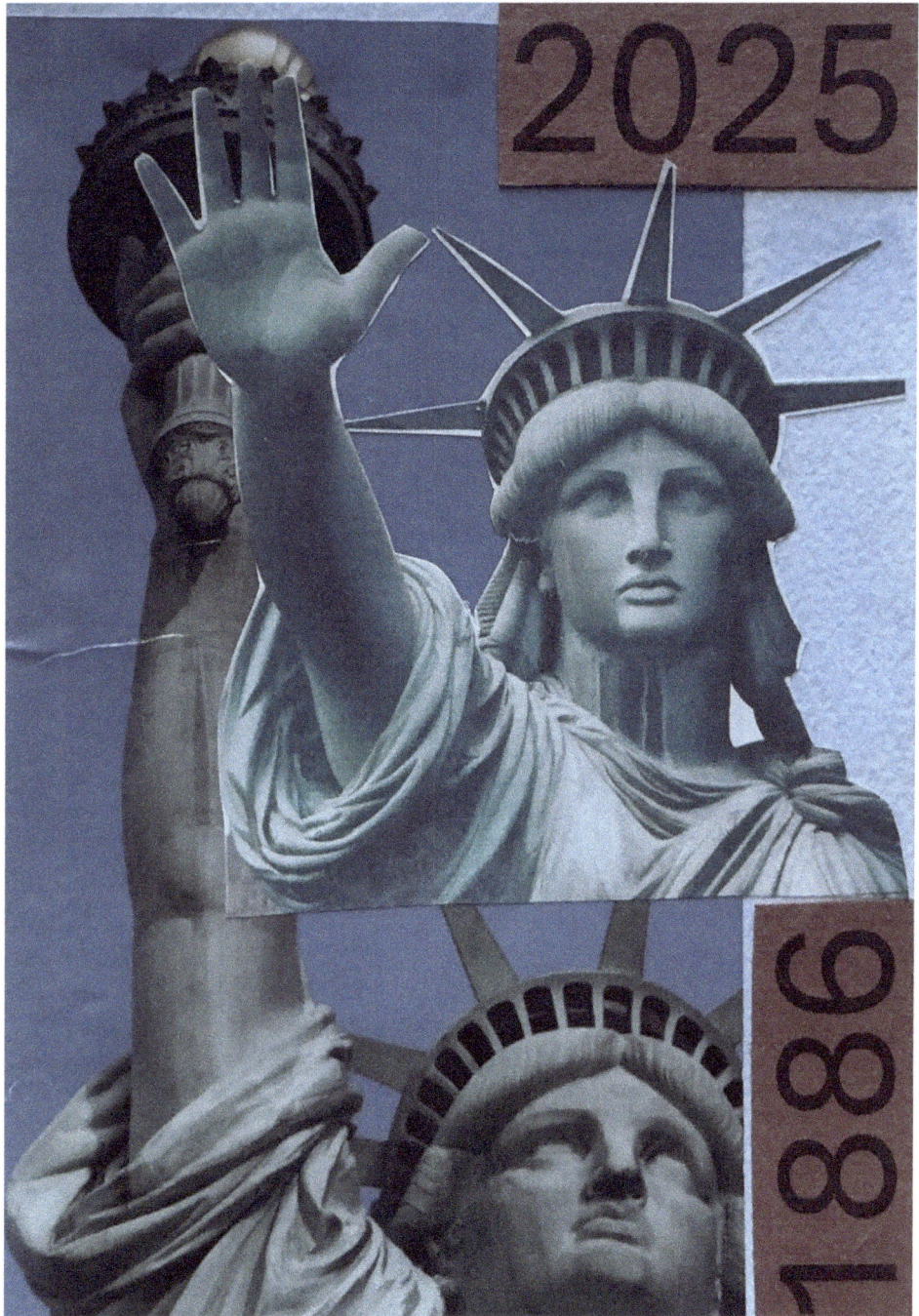

No Entry by Heather Wishik

Wishik juxtaposes an image of the Statue of Liberty with a distorted version where the figure is performing a Sieg Heil salute as a way of commenting on the changing meaning of national symbols. The artist wrote, "Mass deportations and barriers to entry reverse the history of the US and what the statue stands for. The two dates speak to the longevity of the welcome message of the Lady Liberty symbol (even though imperfectly enacted) that the current authoritarians are corrupting through deportation, immigration bans, and highly selective immigration welcomes."

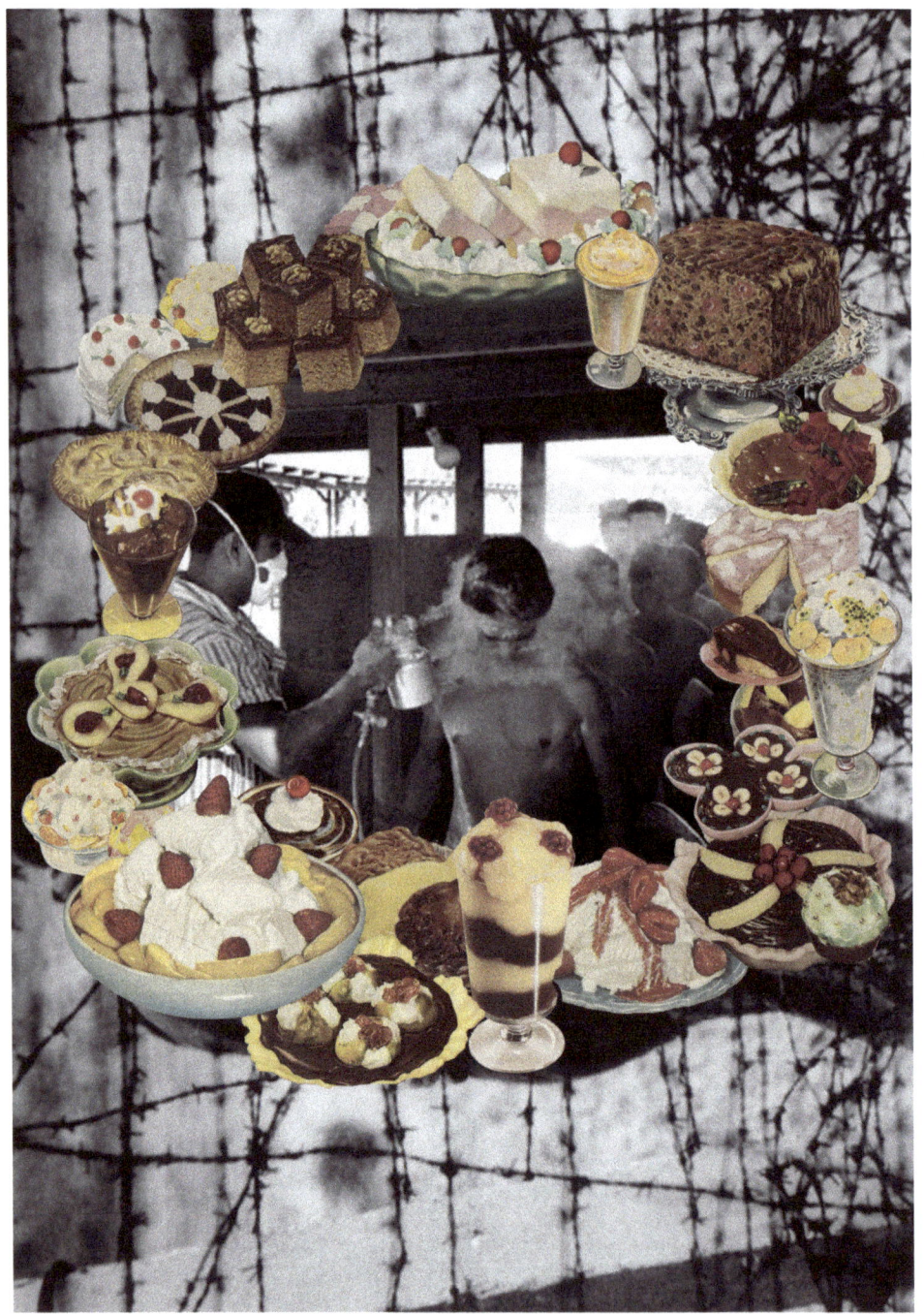

nostalgia (gasoline baths) by Olivia Baldacci

Baldacci places an image of US Border agents dousing naked migrant farm workers with toxic chemicals with a wreath of desserts from 1950s lifestyle magazines. The harsh treatments were part of The Bracero Program which, from 1942 to 1964, oversaw the importation of Mexican laborers to address labor shortages in American agriculture and railroads that were the result of military drafts. The artist wrote, "The role of Mexican immigrants being rewritten as one of inherent criminality, but in reality, they have helped build this country," wrote the artist. "I hope the viewer will consider the consequences of American history on our modern world and how we can fight against history repeating."

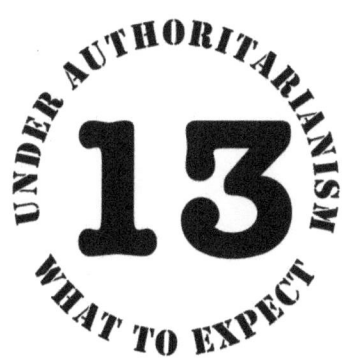

They will try to rewrite history to suit their needs and use the education system to support their agenda. They will smear any historical or living figure who wouldn't approve of their actions, or distort their image to make you think they would.
They will place emphasis on historical education in schools, feeding young minds with the "only correct" version of history and philosophy. They will raise a new generation of voters on their ideology, backing it with a distorted interpretation of history and view of the world.

Guard the education of your children, teach them critical thinking, ensure their openmindedness and protect your real history and heritage.

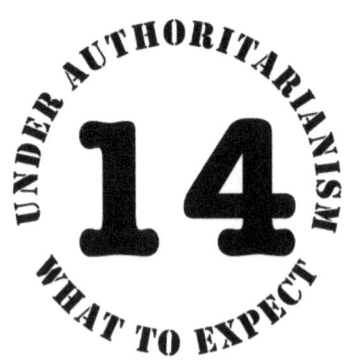

14 — UNDER AUTHORITARIANISM: WHAT TO EXPECT

They will alienate foreign allies and partners, convincing you don't need them.

They won't care for the rest of the world, with their focus on "making your country great again".

While ruining your economy to fulfil their populist promises, they will omit the fact that you're part of a bigger world whose development depends on cooperation, on sharing and on trade.

Don't let them build walls promising you security instead of bridges giving you prosperity.

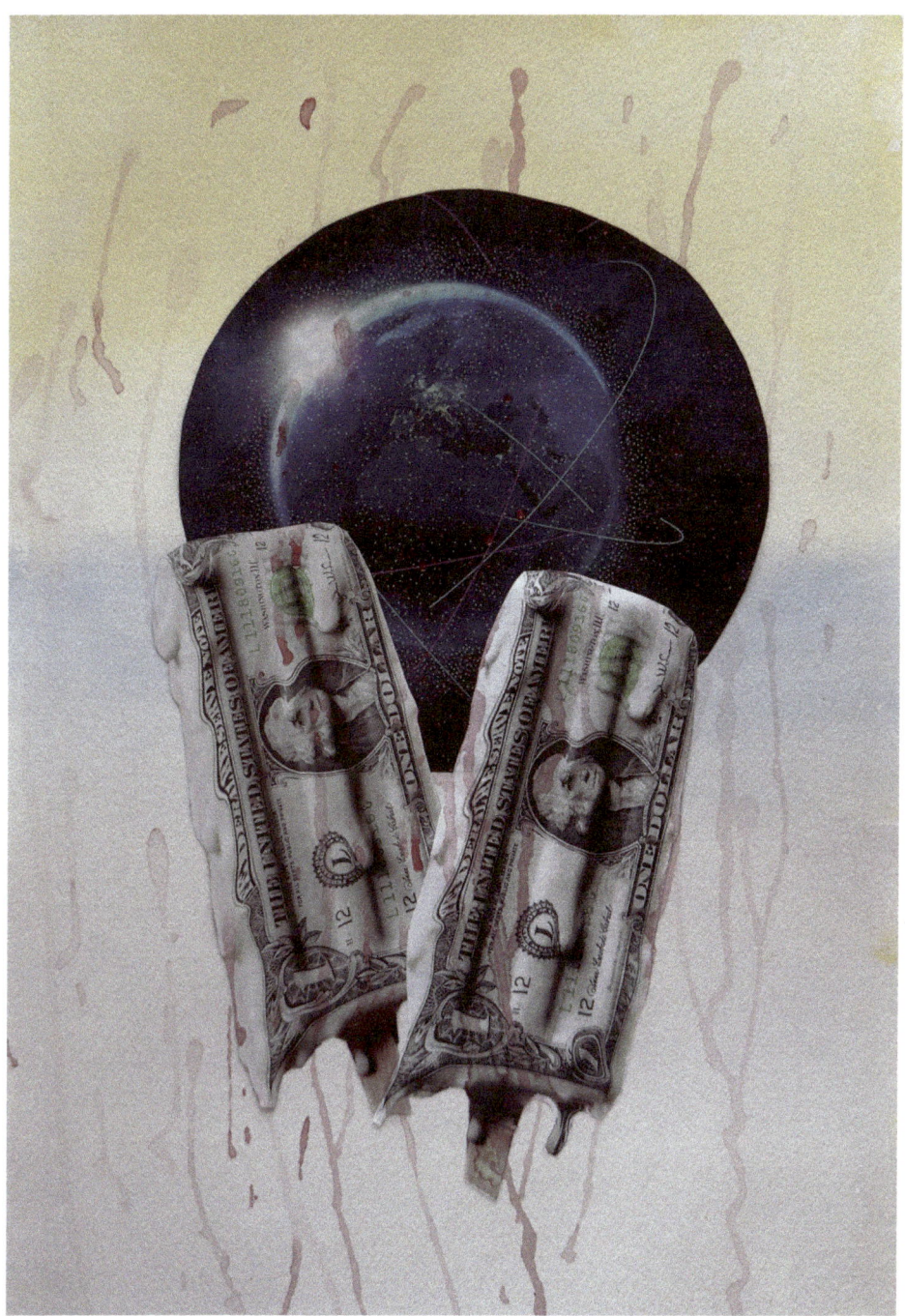

Ruining the Economy by Heather Wishik

Melting US dollars are a warning in Wishik's collage, which itself is a reflection on economic isolationism. The artist described her process, "The combination of the impact of US actions on the world, and the need to remember our membership in a global society, seemed to be the emerging idea. I duplicated the dollar image and laid the dollars over the earth, waiting for the next thought. A pale yellow and blue background for a suggestion of Ukraine came next and the blood drips came last."

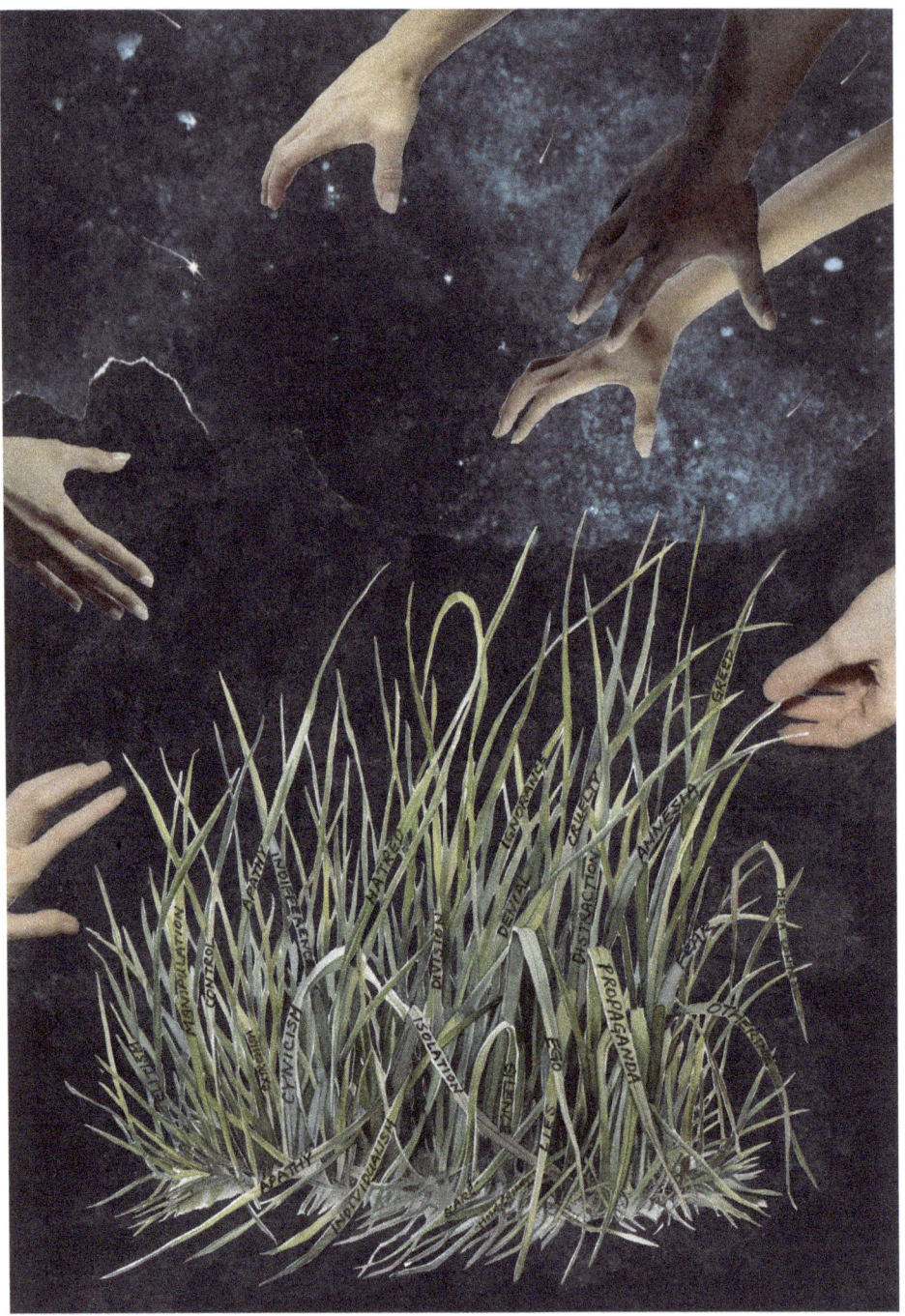

Weeding an Authoritarian Garden by Andrea Lee

Authoritarian regimes can take years and sometimes decades to eventually fall. The artist wrote, "The word 'eventually' can be cold comfort, but it is a reality that must be faced. Rather than a single heroic gesture, a magical moment, or a *deus ex machina*, it is small, quotidian actions done consistently by many hands that will be victorious against the onslaught of authoritarianism. This artwork uses the metaphor of steadily weeding a garden together to prevent the conditions that allow authoritarianism to grow. In fact, though it may feel too late to do these simple actions, but they are still the things that need to be done. No single person can weed the entire garden on their own, but done together, EVENTUALLY, the job will be done."

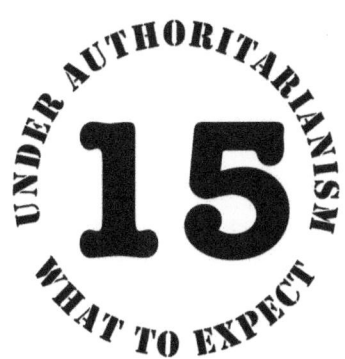

15 — UNDER AUTHORITARIANISM, WHAT TO EXPECT

They will eventually manipulate the electoral system.

They might say it's to correct flaws, to make it more fair, more similar to the rest of the world, or just to make it better.

Don't believe it.

They wouldn't be messing with it at all if it wasn't to benefit them in some way.

> **Oppose any changes to electoral law that an authoritarian regime wants to enact—rest assured it's only to help them remain in power longer.**

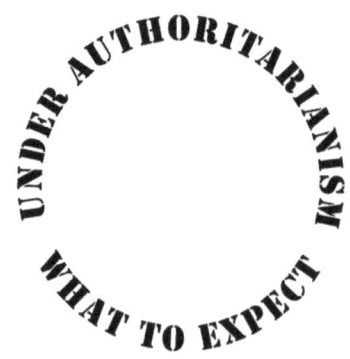

UNDER AUTHORITARIANISM WHAT TO EXPECT

And above all, be strong, fight, endure, and remember you're on the good side of history.

EVERY authoritarian, totalitarian and fascist regime in history eventually failed, thanks to the PEOPLE.

– With love, your Eastern European friends

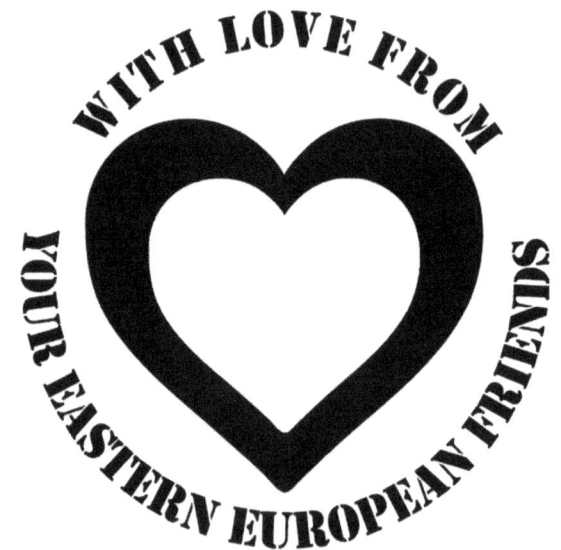

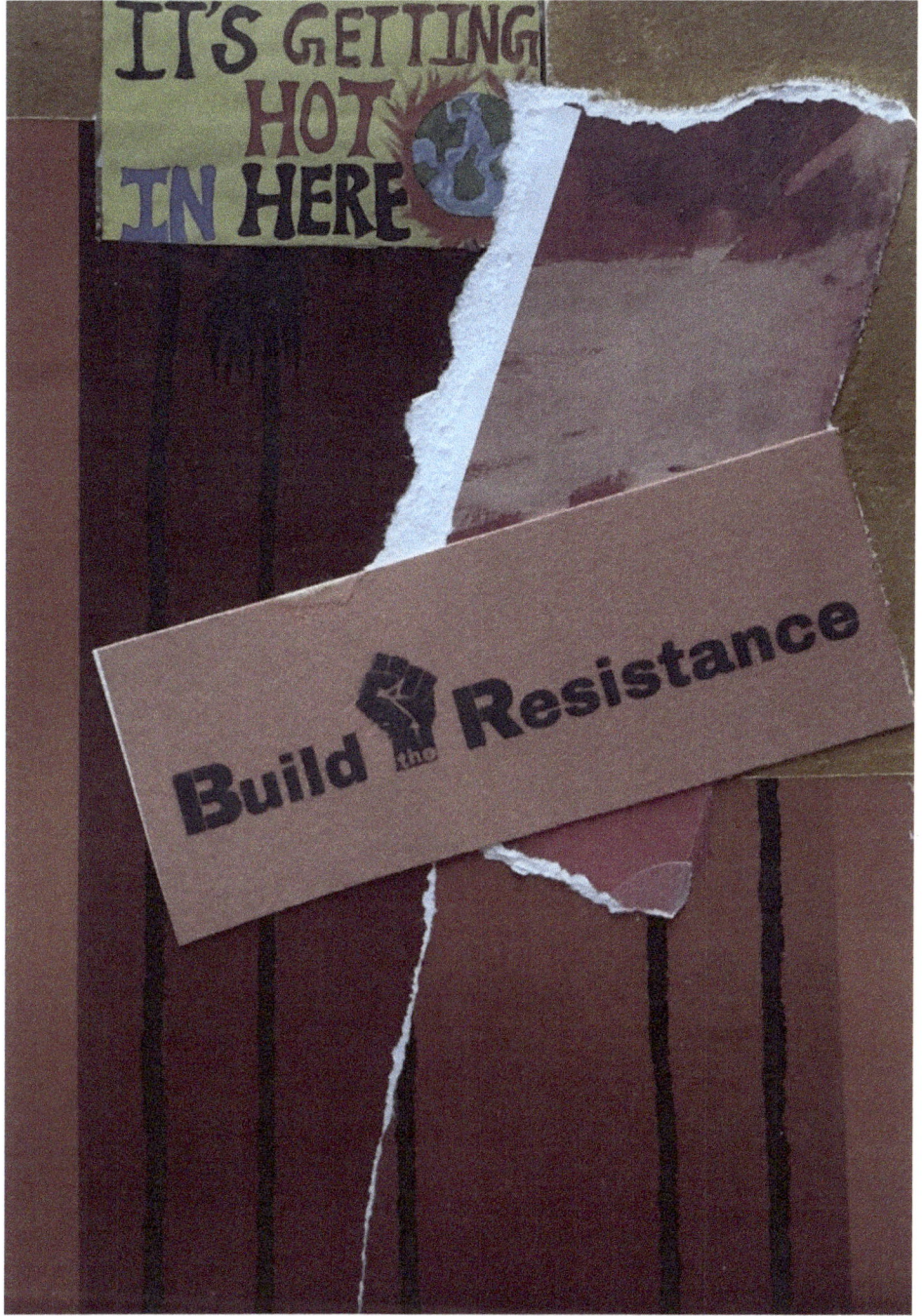

Build the Resistance by Heather Wishik

This collage speaks to the essential response to authoritarianism: resistance. The artist wrote, "As a veteran of the anti-Vietnam War resistance movement and Mobilization to End the War protests at The Pentagon in 1967, I knew I wanted to use the most current resistance logo to build a collage around. The metaphor of the COP 26 sign—that the earth is literally getting hotter, and that politics are heating up now under spreading authoritarianism, struck me as useful. Then I wanted to heat up the collage with are related colors for the backdrop."

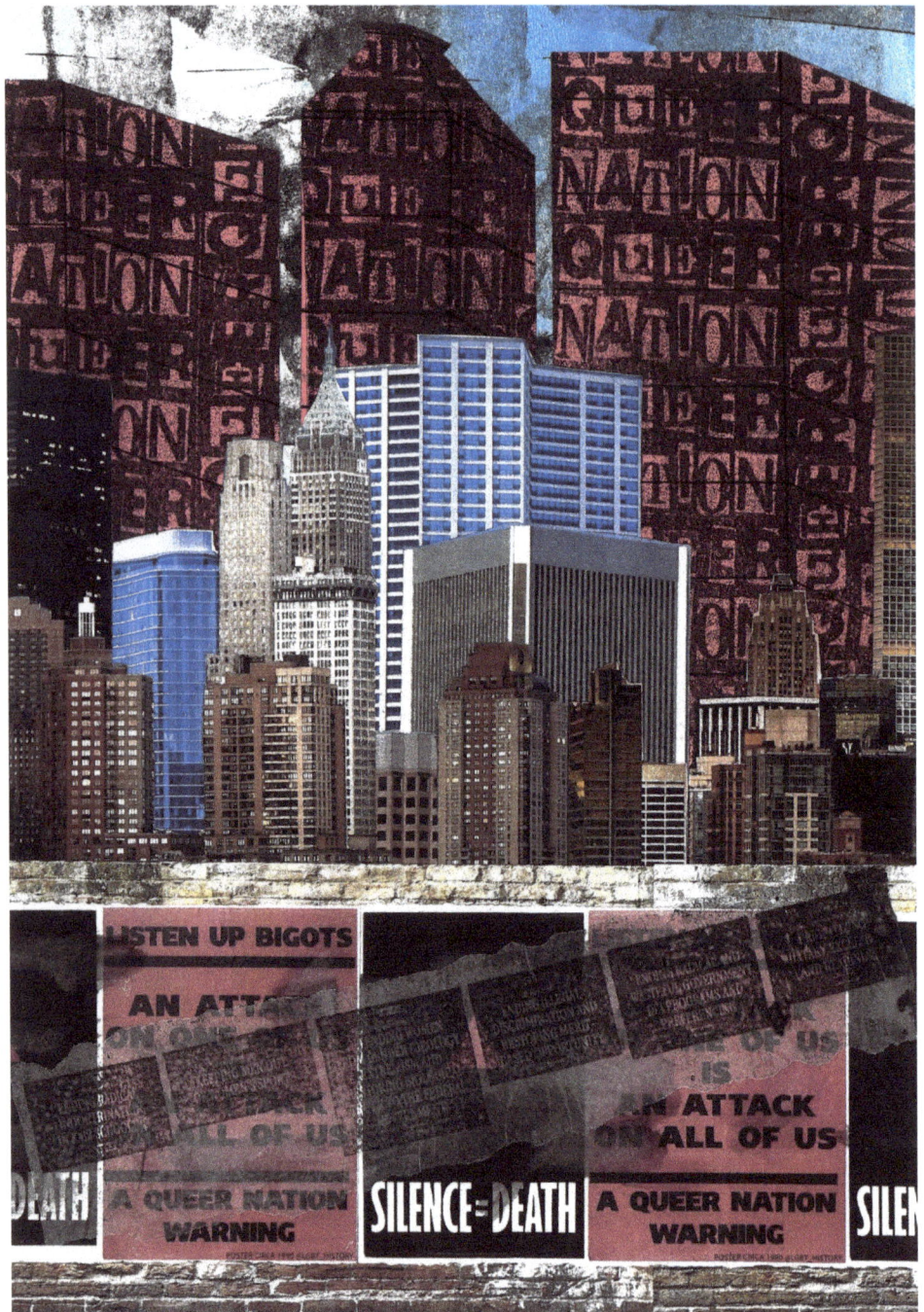

Everything Old Is New Again by Jennifer R Myhre

The artist wrote, "Queer Nation was a direct action group in the early 1990s responding both to gay bashing and the federal government's willingness to let LGBTQ people die during the AIDS crisis. It rejected respectability politics and followed in the footsteps of other queer groups who had reappropriated, as a symbol of power, the pink triangle used by the Nazis to try to humiliate gay men in concentration camps. This collage draws on posters used by Queer Nation in the 1990s and overlays them with the executive orders by President Trump in 2025 that roll back civil liberties for queer and trans people."

AUTHORITARIAN CHECKLIST

AUTHORITARIAN

- ☐ Win elections on fear & populist promises

- ☐ Reclaim power for the People from the "elites"

- ☐ Purge highest positions in key government institutions

- ☐ Place cronies in positions of highest power regardless of their competence

- ☐ Brush off any critical press as "fake", "corrupt", "acting against the People"

- ☐ Bluntly lie to the People

- ☐ Ban press from parliament/congress/White House or selectively limit their access

- ☐ Limit press freedom & quietly take control of mainstream media

CHECKLIST

☐ Label opposition & protesters as "traitors", "elites trying to reclaim power"

☐ Limit freedom of assembly

☐ Fix highest court to be able to bypass Constitution "for the good of the people"

☐ Limit minority & women's rights

☐ Ruin the economy to fulfil your populist promises in the short term

☐ Alienate international partners and allies, "making your country great again"

☐ Quietly fix electoral law under the disguise of making it better

☐ Start over, until there's nothing left...

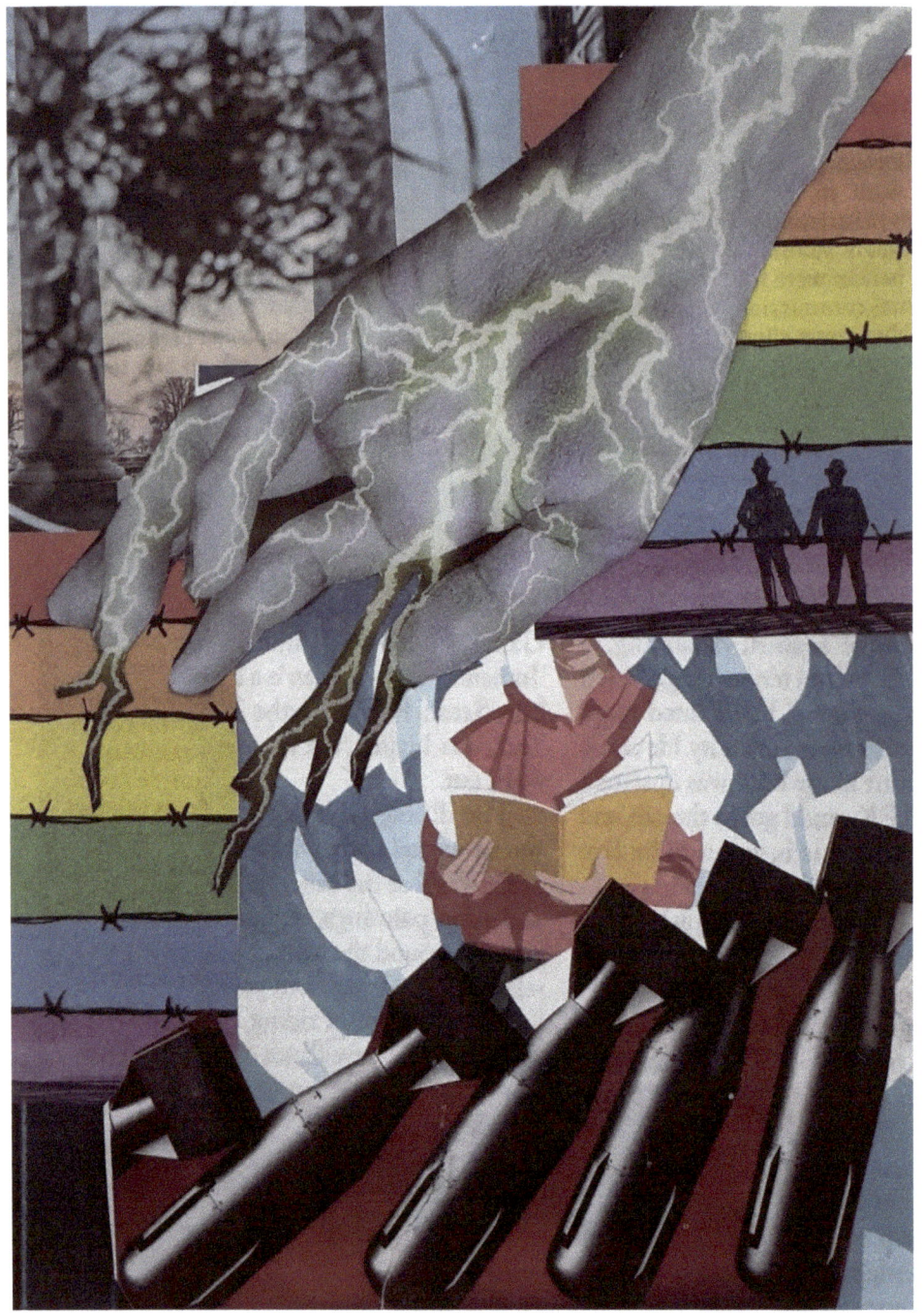

They Will Create Chaos by Heather Wishik

"The hand with the lightning bolt suggests chaos created, as do the pages flying around. The bombs suggest warmongering. Rainbow flags suggest the anti-LGBTQ policies of authoritarians including Victor Orban, Vladimir Putin, Donald Trump, and Elon Musk, and how these are framed as protective of children and parents," wrote the artist. "This emerged from play with saved materials. I saw the hand with the lightning bolts emerging from the fingers in my collection of magazine papers. The rest evolved as I sorted through my papers. The bullet hole in the Capitol window and the bombs indicate danger. The person trying to read with pages flying around suggests chaos, book banning and censorship."

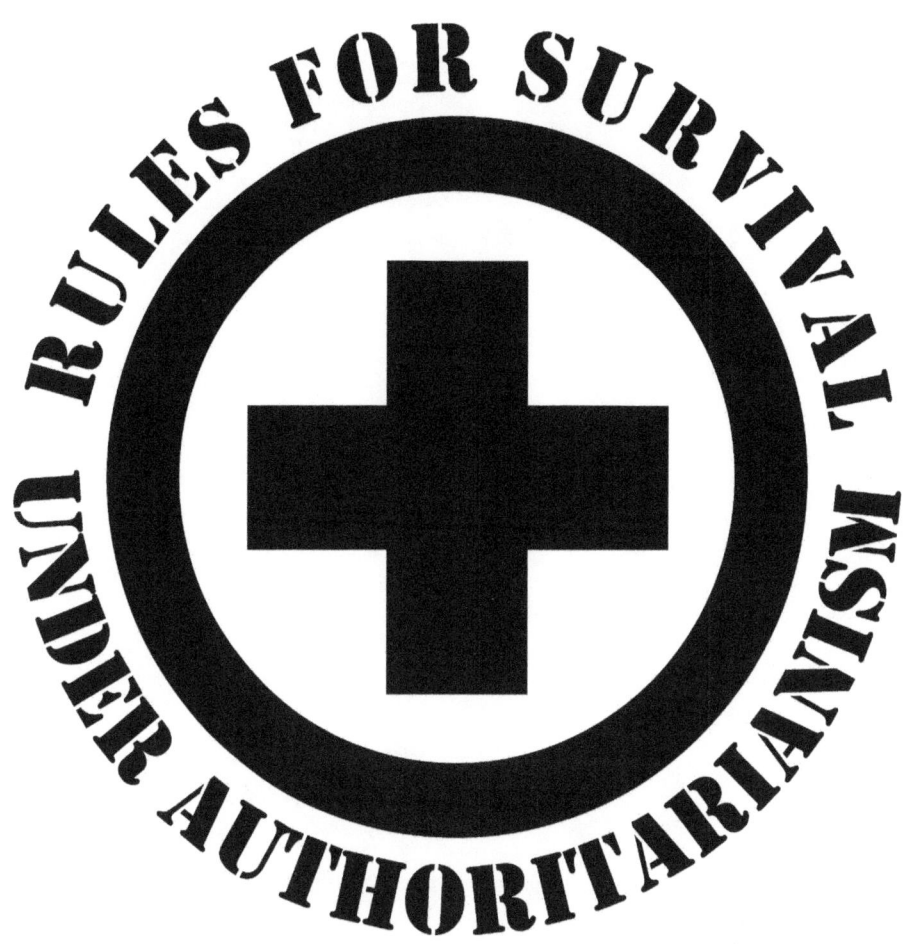

Authoritarianism doesn't last.
How to make it through?

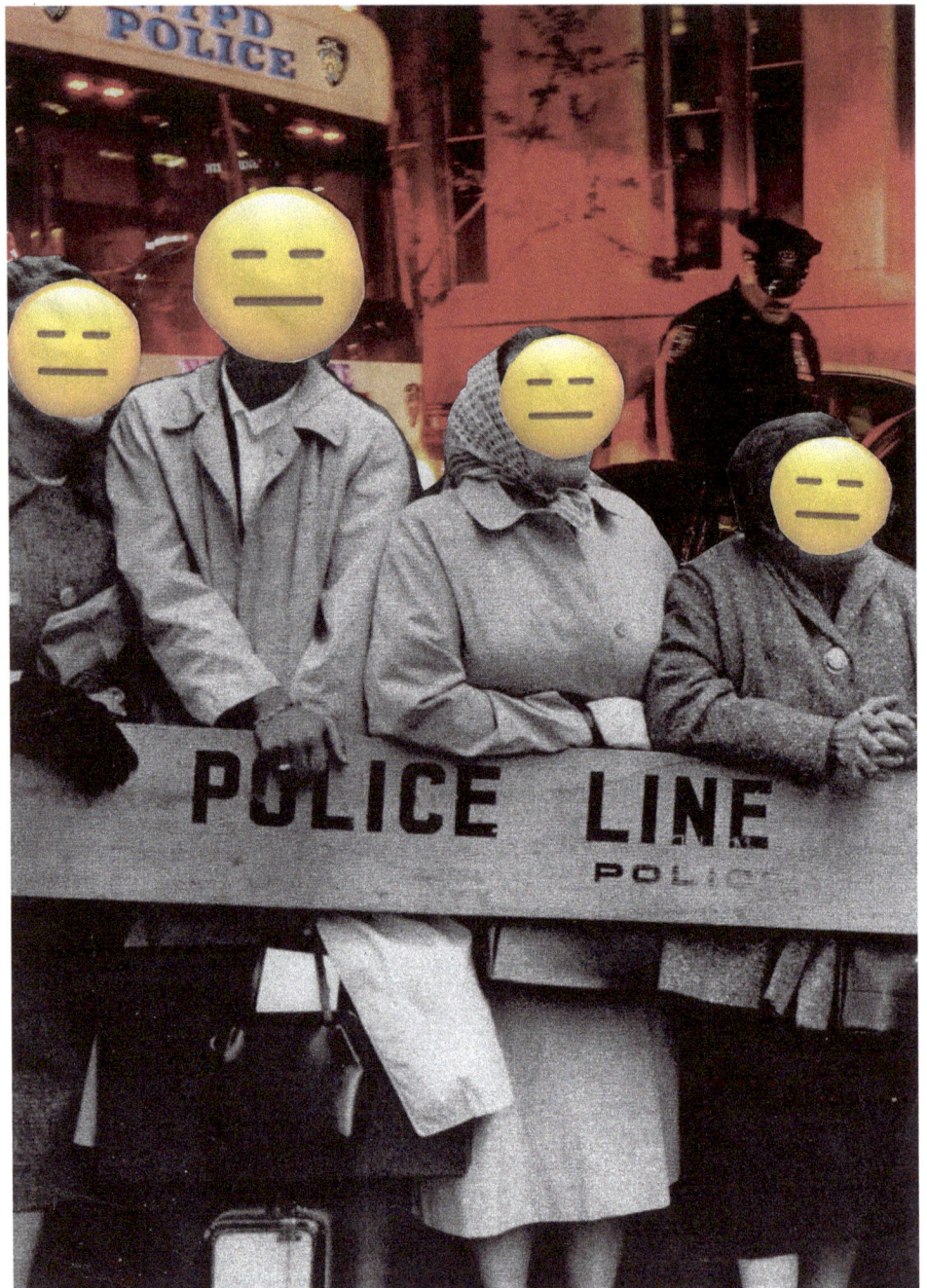

The Bystanders by Lori Petchers

Petchers places apathy emojis over the faces of four women waiting to see Nikita Khrushchev behind a police barricade in front of Waldorf-Astoria in New York City on 17 September 1959. "To overcome authoritarianism, we must be engaged," said the artist, who further contextualized the collage with a quote from Elie Wiesel, "We must take sides. Neutrality helps the oppressor, never the victim. Silence encourages the tormentor, never the tormented. Sometimes we must interfere. When human lives are endangered, when human dignity is in jeopardy, national borders and sensitivities become irrelevant. Wherever men and women are persecuted because of their race, religion, or political views, that place must—at that moment—become the center of the universe."

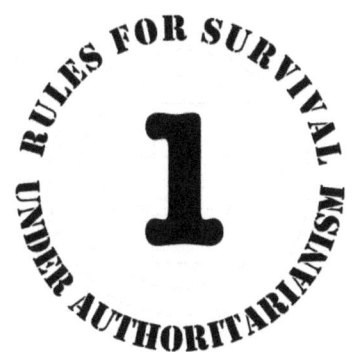

Don't stay indifferent.

It WILL concern you eventually.

It will concern your family, your friends.

Voice your objection
IMMEDIATELY.

Show them you care. RESIST.

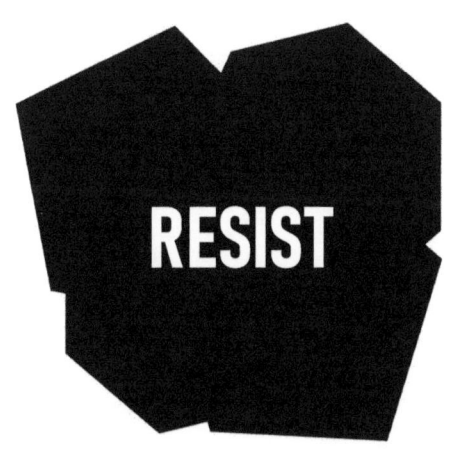

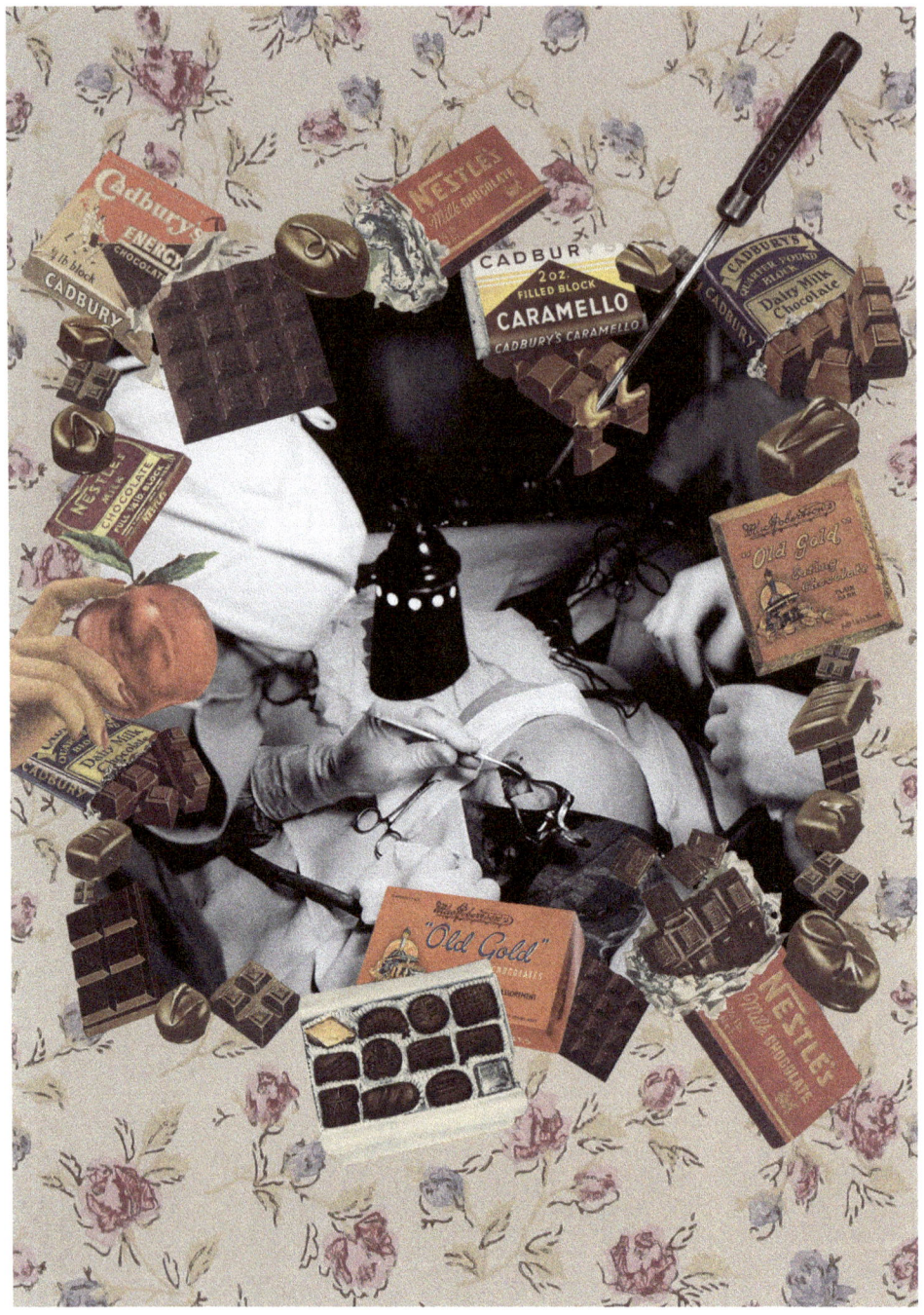

nostalgia (lobotomy) **by Olivia Baldacci**

In her characteristic style, Baldacci juxtaposes chocolate candy with surgical lobotomy as an invitation to meditate on how authoritarian states thrive on fear and ignorance. The artist wrote, "The central black and white image is a doctor performing a lobotomy on an unnamed patient in the 1940s. The background is a vintage wallpaper pattern, with a photo frame composed of chocolate bars, boxes, and wrappers. The ice pick in the top right corner, a tool that doctors used for lobotomies, symbolizes the wrath of the authoritarian state in forcing its people to all think one way. My goal is for viewers to question the information their leaders are spreading. Is this information all emotion based? Is there evidence to back up their claims?"

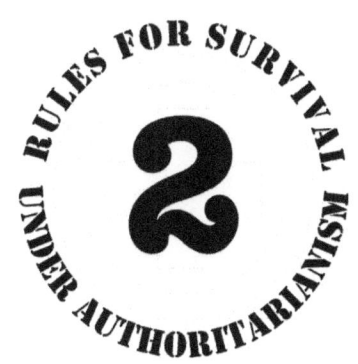

They thrive on FEAR & IGNORANCE.

Expose their scaremongering, show flaws in their arguments.

Raise awareness, EDUCATE people around you.

They will try to distort FACTS, rewrite history.

DON'T LET THEM.

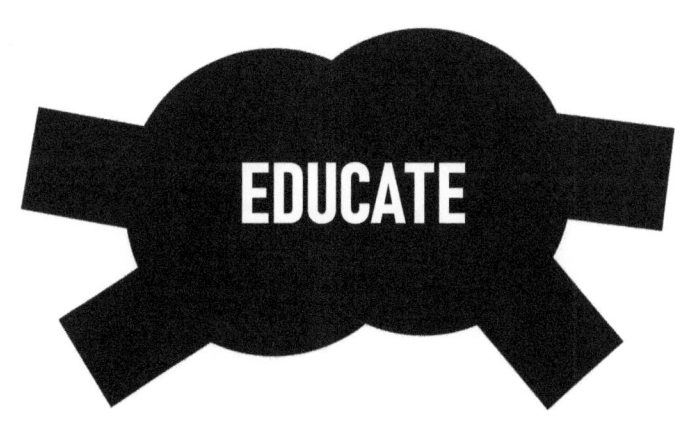

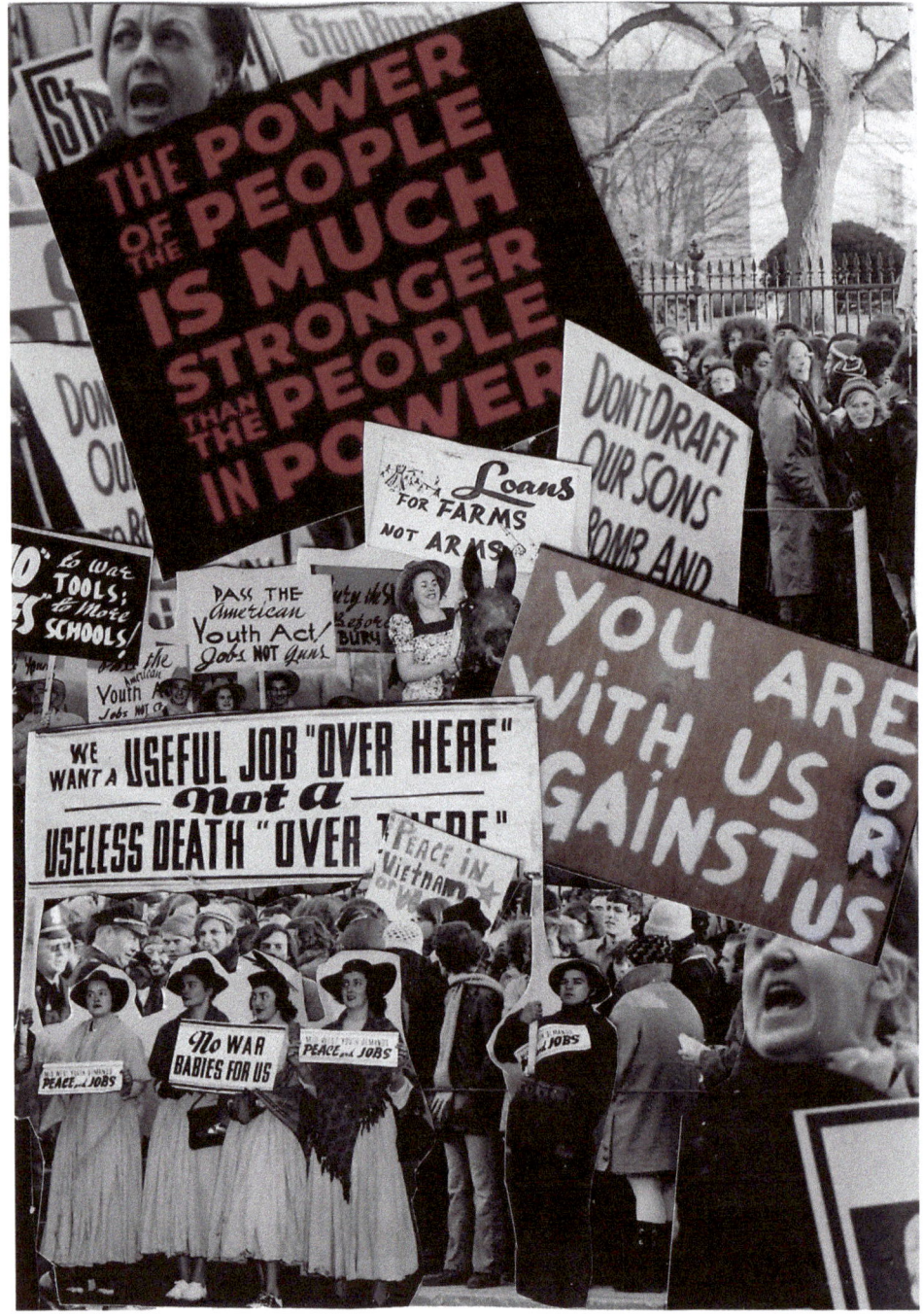

Power to the People by Lori Petchers

Petchers collages contemporary images of protest with those found in the Library of Congress to give us an image of people taking to the streets in opposition to authoritarianism. The artist wrote, "The combination of protests about different issues and from different time periods juxtaposed with contemporary posters, remind the viewer that our voices are important. We must exercise our Freedom of Speech and use our Right of Assembly to advocate for what is right and just. Authoritarian governments want to silence the people, but it is up to the people to overthrow the oppressors. Peaceful protest is one of our most time tested and effective tools. I hope the viewer will be inspired to continue the historic tradition of protest."

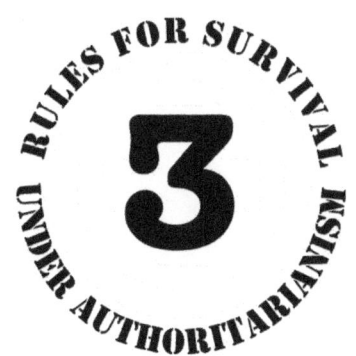

Organize protest movements, mobilize civil society.

They're well organized, so should you be.

FLOOD THE STREETS.

They WILL back off when they see your numbers.

They depend on you – the PEOPLE.

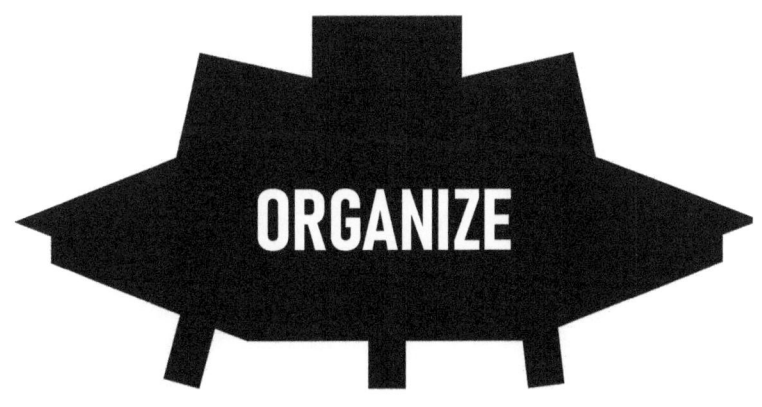

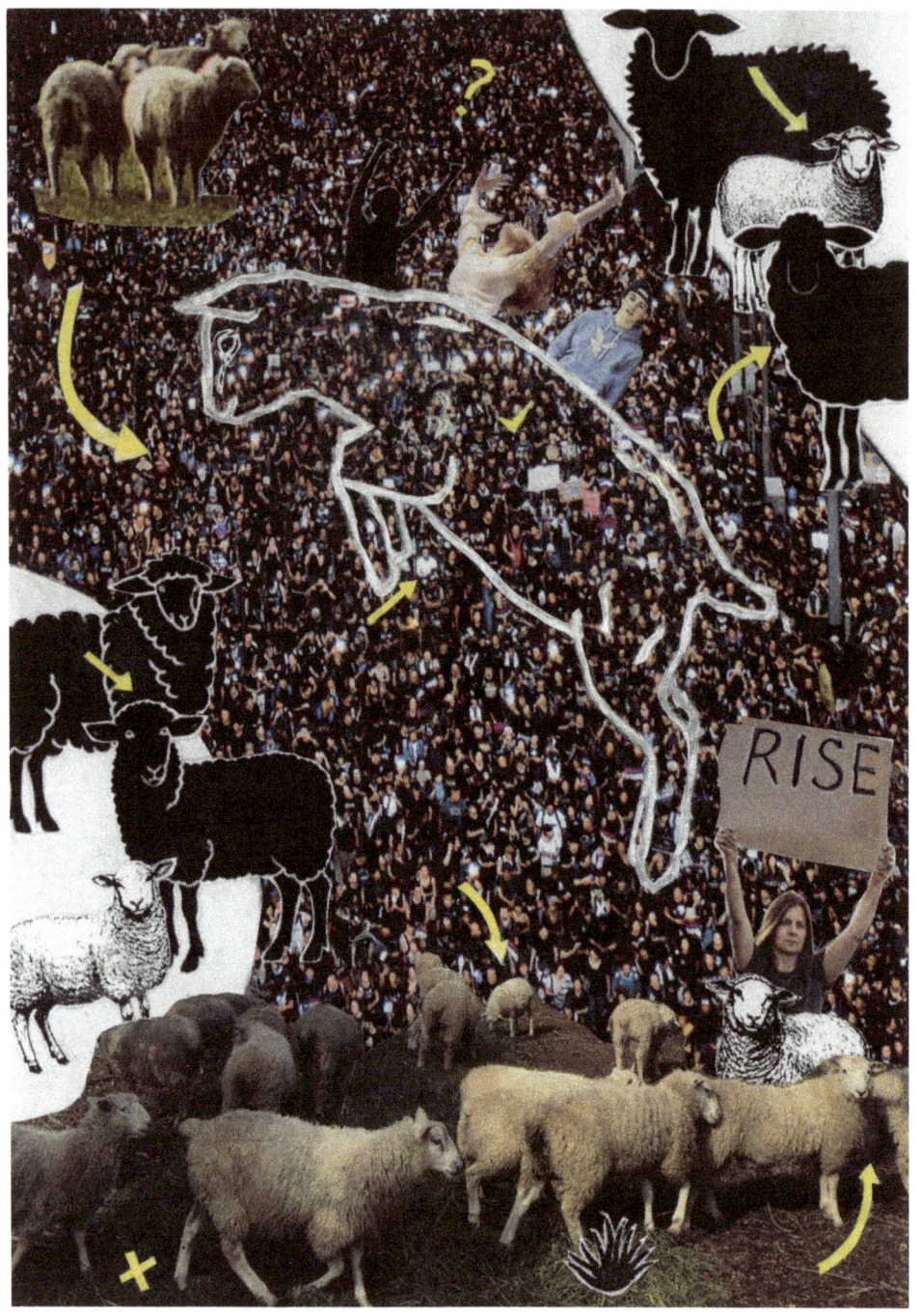

Where are you in the Sheepscape? by Andrea Lee

Lee invites a moment of self-reflection on apathy in this collage that combines images of sheep, crowds, and protests. Part of a diptych, the panel seen here "shows what a crowd of action takers would look like, if they would only risk taking the leap. We also see the questioning and wondering entailed in deciding to rise up." The artist wrote, "These works speak to the issue of apathy and bystander syndrome, whereby large numbers of individuals refrain from taking action, hoping to avoid getting involved in the messy, chaotic and sometimes violent or dangerous process of combatting authoritarianism. Following the safety of the herd, and obediently doing or believing whatever an authoritarian leader says to do or believe, is what sheep do."

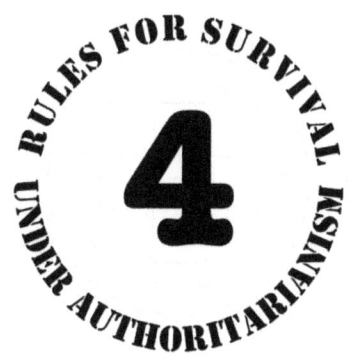

Don't let them DIVIDE you into different classes of citizens, "true Americans", "patriots" vs "traitors", "enemies of the state".

You're ALL citizens, ONE nation, despite different beliefs and ideology.

Make your diversity your STRENGTH.

Stay TOGETHER for a common goal – survival of your country, of freedom and democracy.

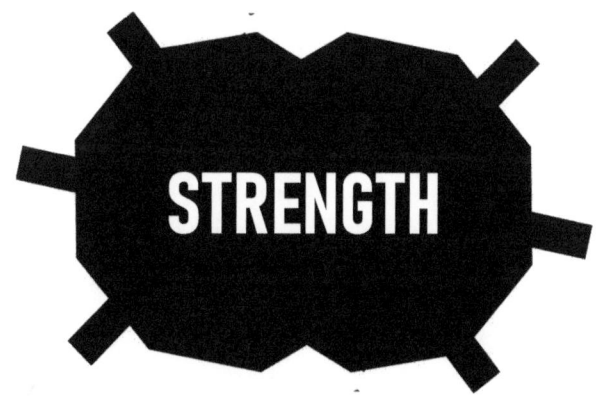

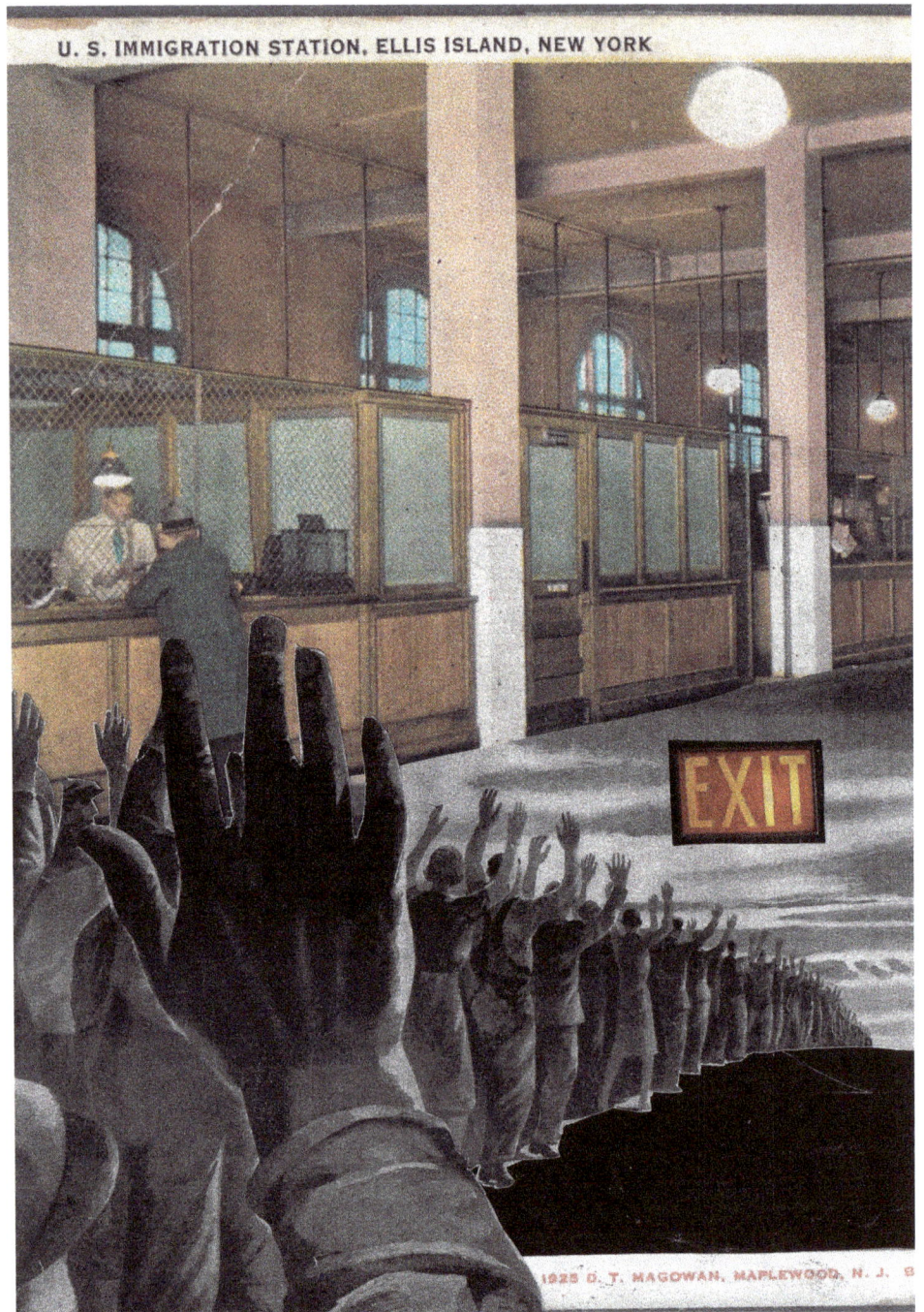

Exit Through the Gift Shop by Lori Petchers

Petchers intervenes on a 1925 postcard of the Immigration station at Ellis Island found in the New York Public Library archives. The artist wrote, "The date is significant since The Immigration Act of 1924, also known as the Johnson-Reed Act, which severely restricted immigration to the United States, went into effect in 1925. This postcard was probably a typical souvenir one would buy at a gift shop in New York City at the time...My parents came through Ellis Island from Eastern Europe in 1950 after the Holocaust, and greatly benefitted from the ability to immigrate. Authoritarian governments demonize foreigners and often restrict immigration under this guise of protecting the 'real' citizens."

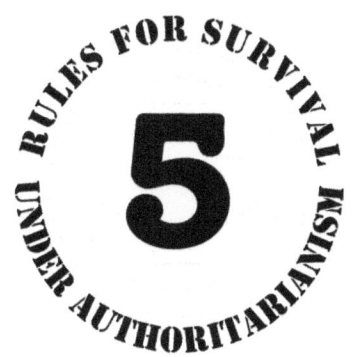

Don't give up, don't get tired, and don't try to wait it out.

Don't hope it will pass.

It WON'T.

They will manipulate the people, control the media to sway public opinion, fix the electoral system and STAY FOR GOOD.

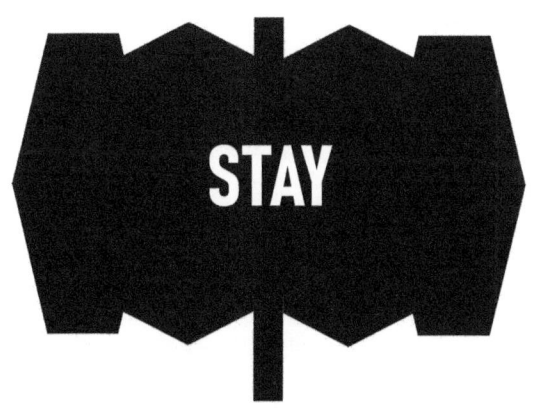

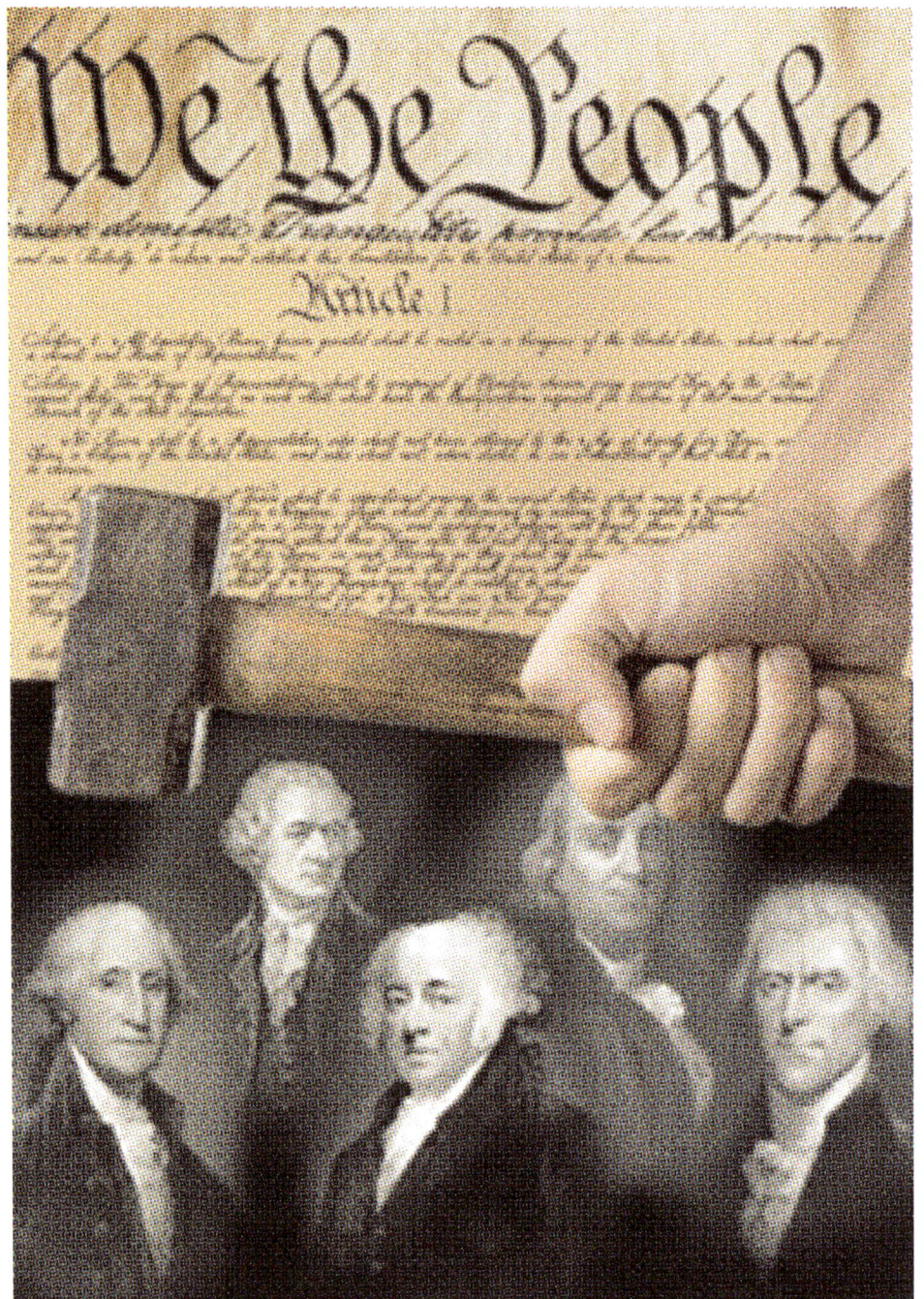

Founders Smash or The Smash of Rights by Suzanne Gore

The artist wrote, "This collage illustrates the smashing of the rights of citizens of the United States of America. The image evolved from several different drawings of gavels—thinking that would show the laws of the land being destroyed, but I settled on a photo of a hand and a sledgehammer as an image to more accurately illustrate the point of the collage. This collage addresses taking over National Symbols as well as denial and destruction of the bedrock of the founding of American Democracy. It speaks to the disrespect and disregard for the freedoms that should be held most dear and, hopefully, supports the rights of the citizens of the United States of America."

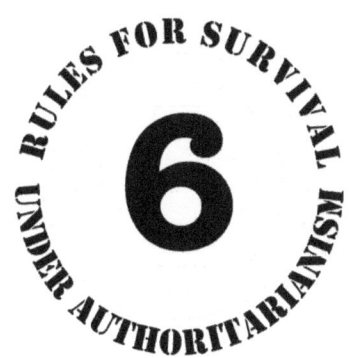

6
RULES FOR SURVIVAL UNDER AUTHORITARIANISM

If you don't get them to back off or to step down, you better make goddamn SURE that when the next elections come, assuming there's still any democracy left, NO ONE will vote for the same bastard(s) again!

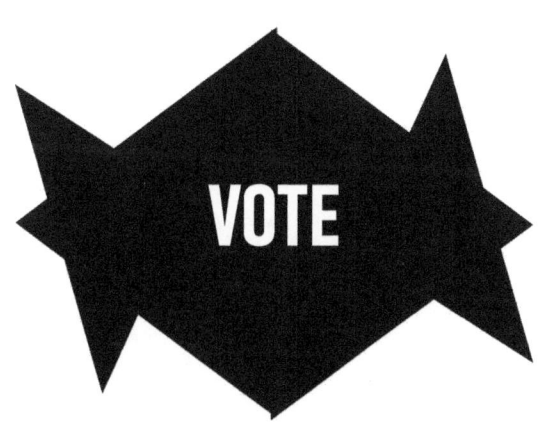

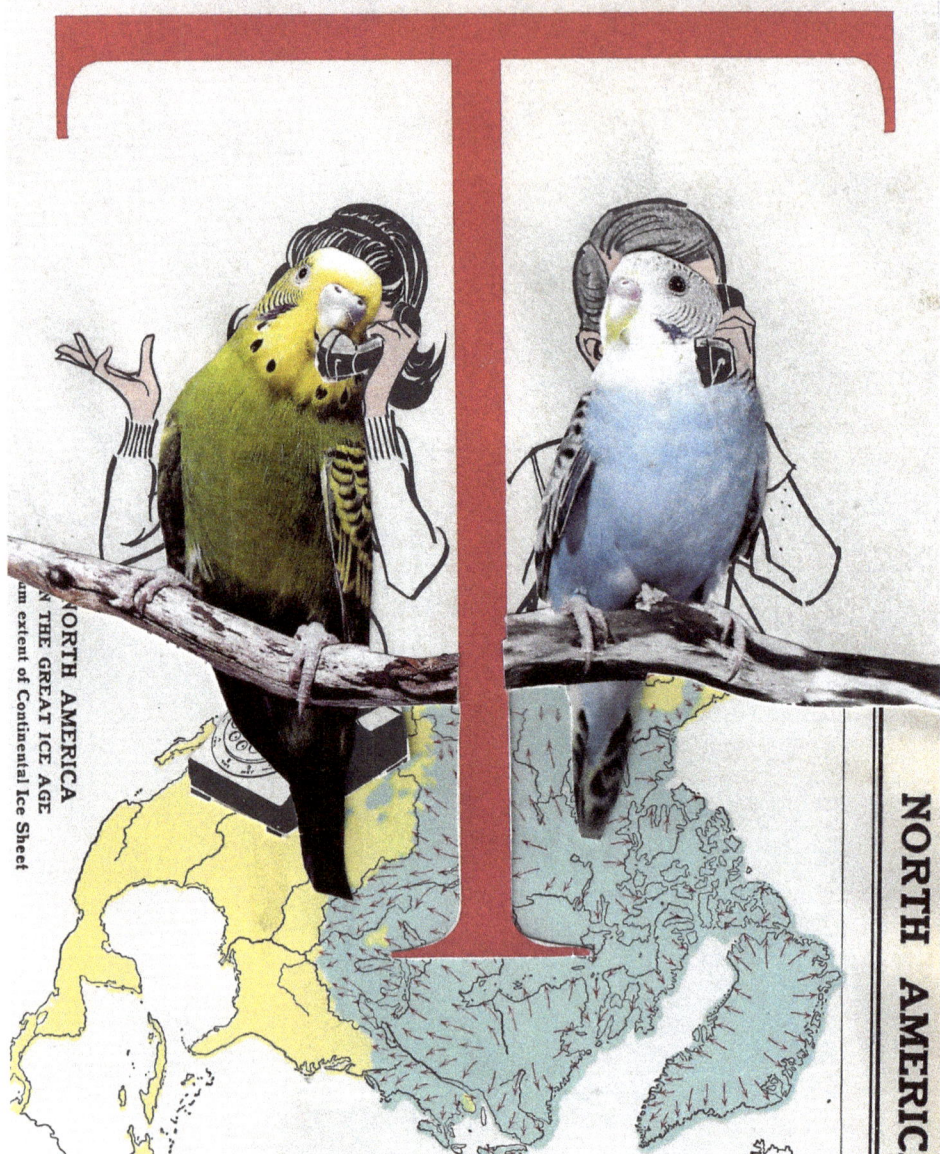

Polly Wants a Conversation by Lori Petchers

Petchers collages over the chatty figures on an old telephone instruction pamphlet with birds as a reminder of how it is important to talk to others about authoritarianism. The artist wrote, "Using a bit of humor, this collage reminds us in order to save democracy we must talk with one another and remember our shared interests. The telephone eliminated distance as a communication obstacle, but perhaps in our fully connected world we now have other obstacles we need to overcome. The phone can be used to communicate instead of agitate. Authoritarian governments want the people to stay divided. It is important to overcome our differences and respect each other."

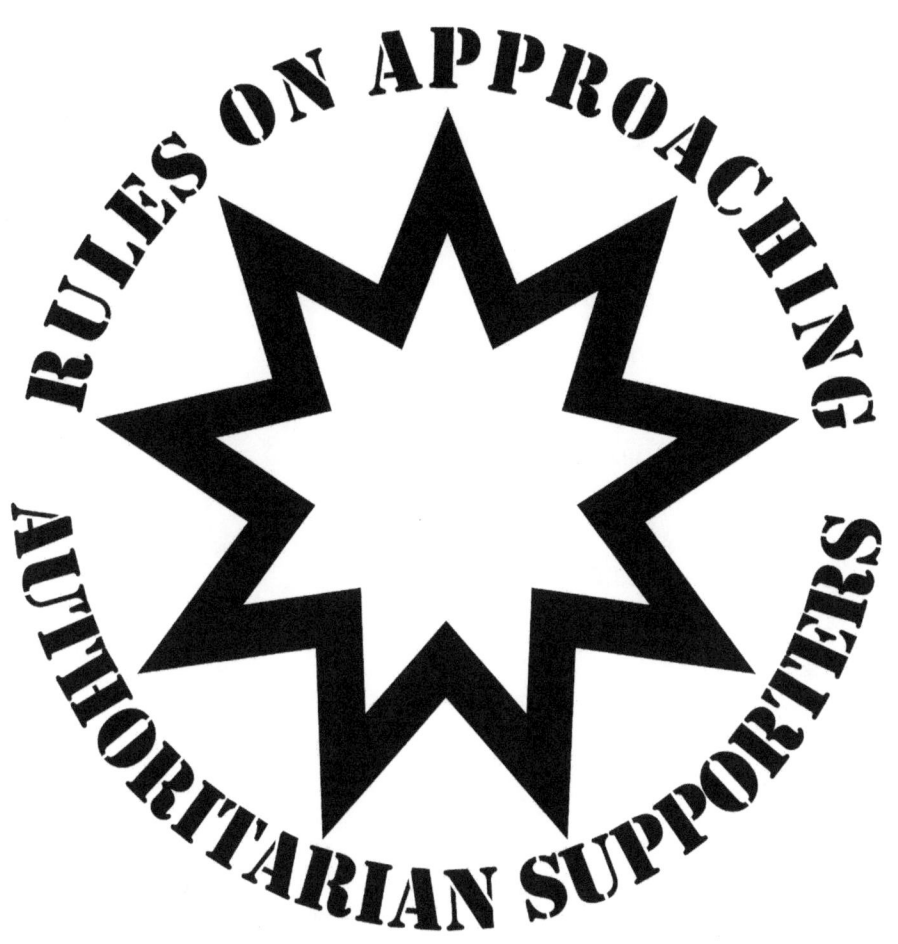

RULES ON APPROACHING AUTHORITARIAN SUPPORTERS

What if your neighbor, friend or family member supports the authoritarian regime?

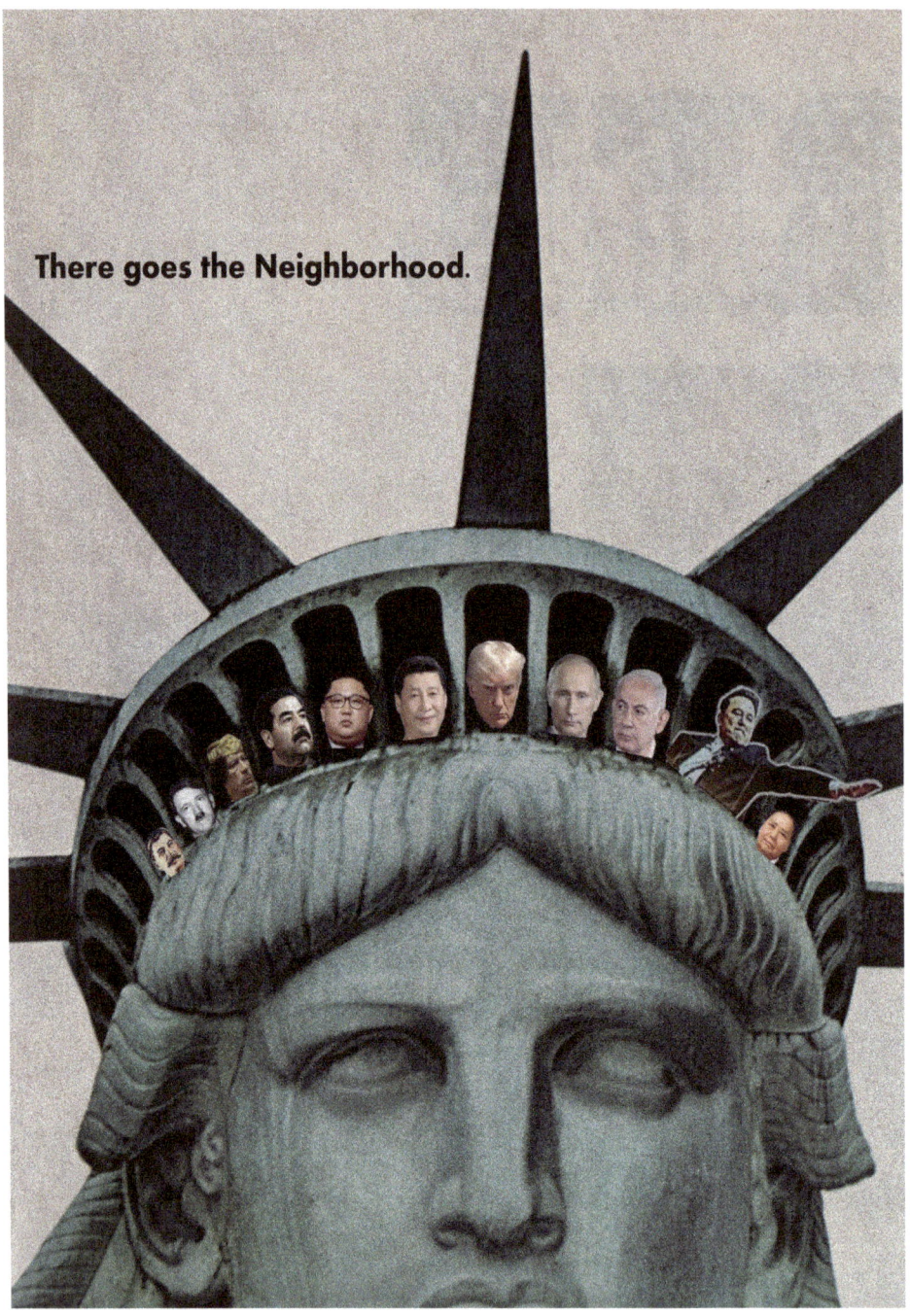

There Goes the Neighborhood by Suzanne Gore

Gore places the heads of dictators in the crown of the Statue of Liberty. The artist wrote, "'There goes the neighborhood' is a colloquial phrase that expresses disapproval of something or someone that has negatively impacted a neighborhood. It often implies a change in the neighborhood's social or economic makeup. In this case, it refers to the rise of current and past authoritarianism and illustrates how dictators destroy freedom and lives by control and perhaps genocide. This collage illustrates how dictators use power and control to 'get into our heads' in the sense that people may dwell, analyze, and worry excessively about them."

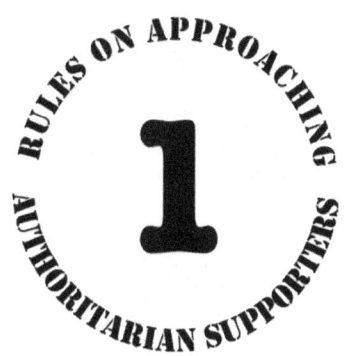

RULES ON APPROACHING AUTHORITARIAN SUPPORTERS — 1

Don't look down on them, don't patronize them, even if you know what they're saying has no factual basis or you find it offensive.

Don't preach, ask questions.

Try to understand them, where they are coming from, what their problems are and why they see solutions to them in the regime.

Treat them as people, as equals.

They believe what they're saying is true and they might have valid reasons for their support.

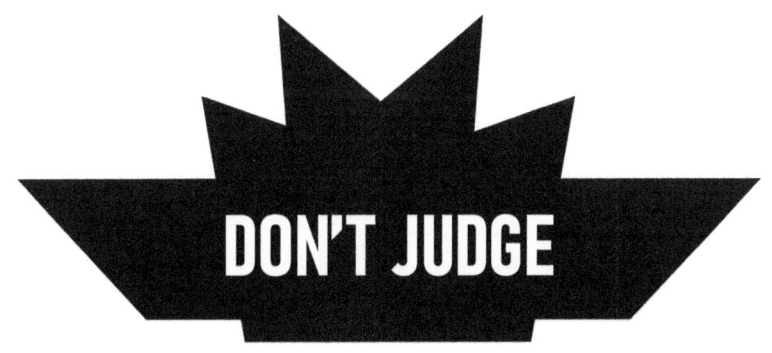

DON'T JUDGE

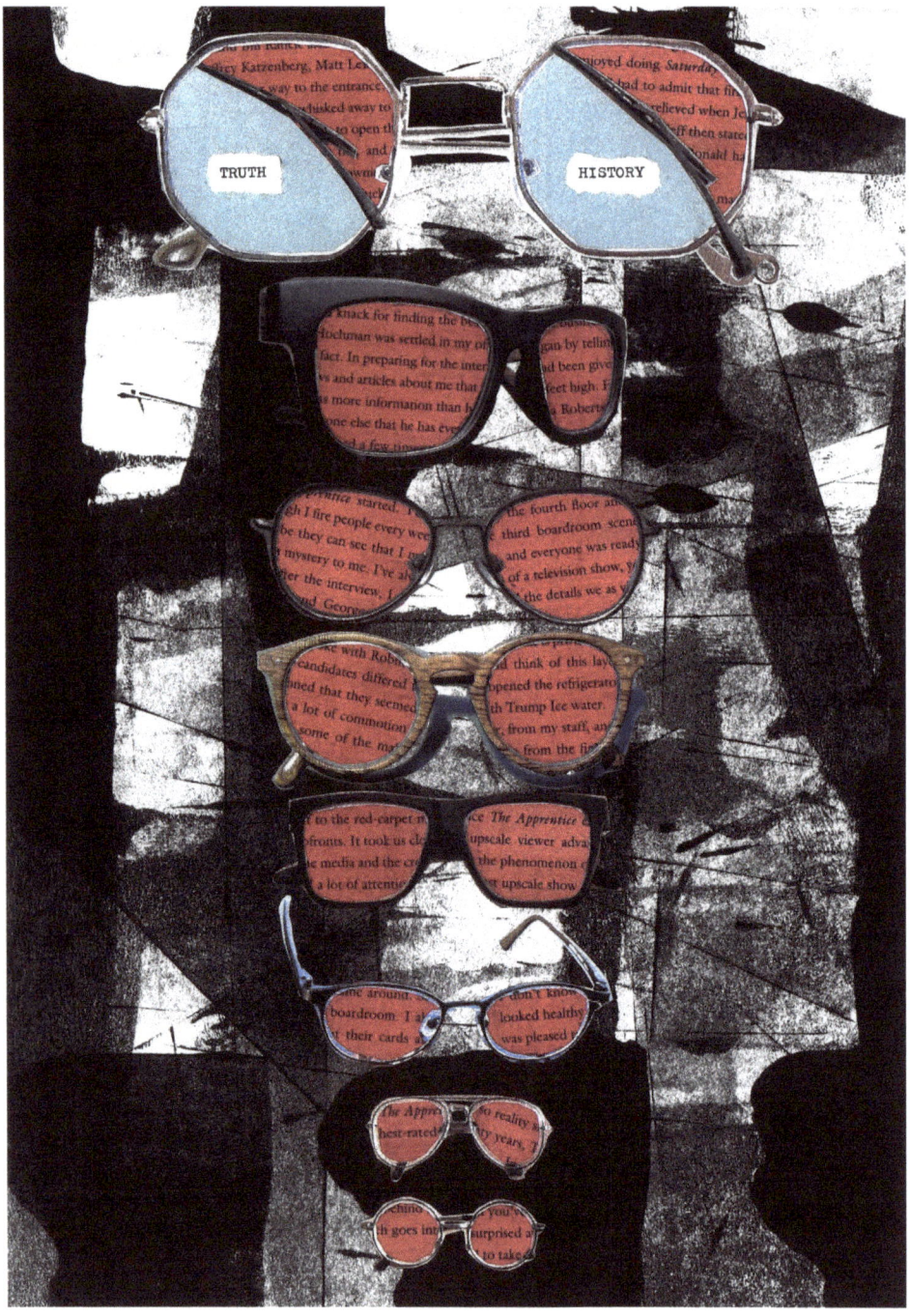

Seeing Red by Jennifer R Myhre

The artist wrote, "The text printed over in red in the eyeglasses is from Donald Trump's *How to Think Like a Billionaire* and the pages are a blow by blow account of the day to day experience he had while filming *The Apprentice*. This collage points to the use of spectacle as a distraction, but also used by Trump (and other authoritarians) as a rage-generator, both for his supporters and for his opposition, and the ways in which that rage gets in the way of seeing clearly."

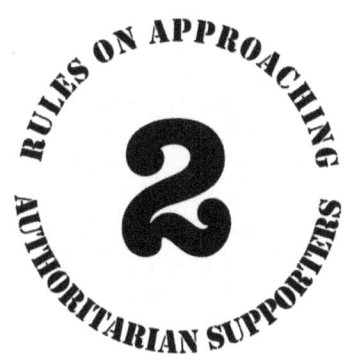

Don't get emotional, don't get provoked into heated arguments.

Fight the other side's emotions with your calm, logical approach.

The angrier they get, the calmer you should be.

They'll calm down eventually.

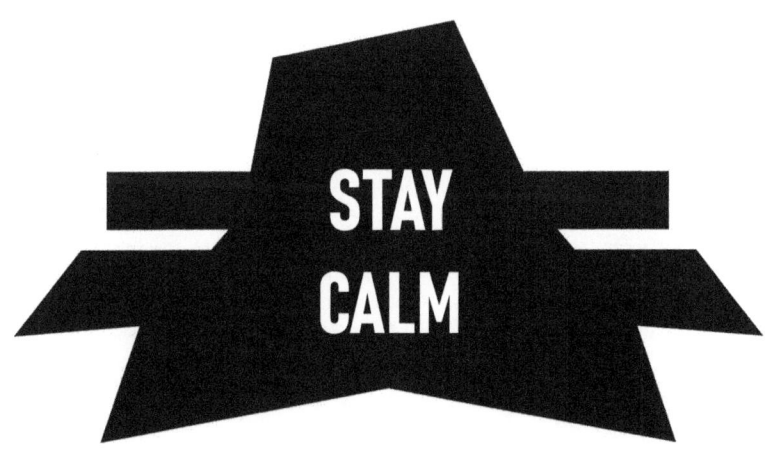

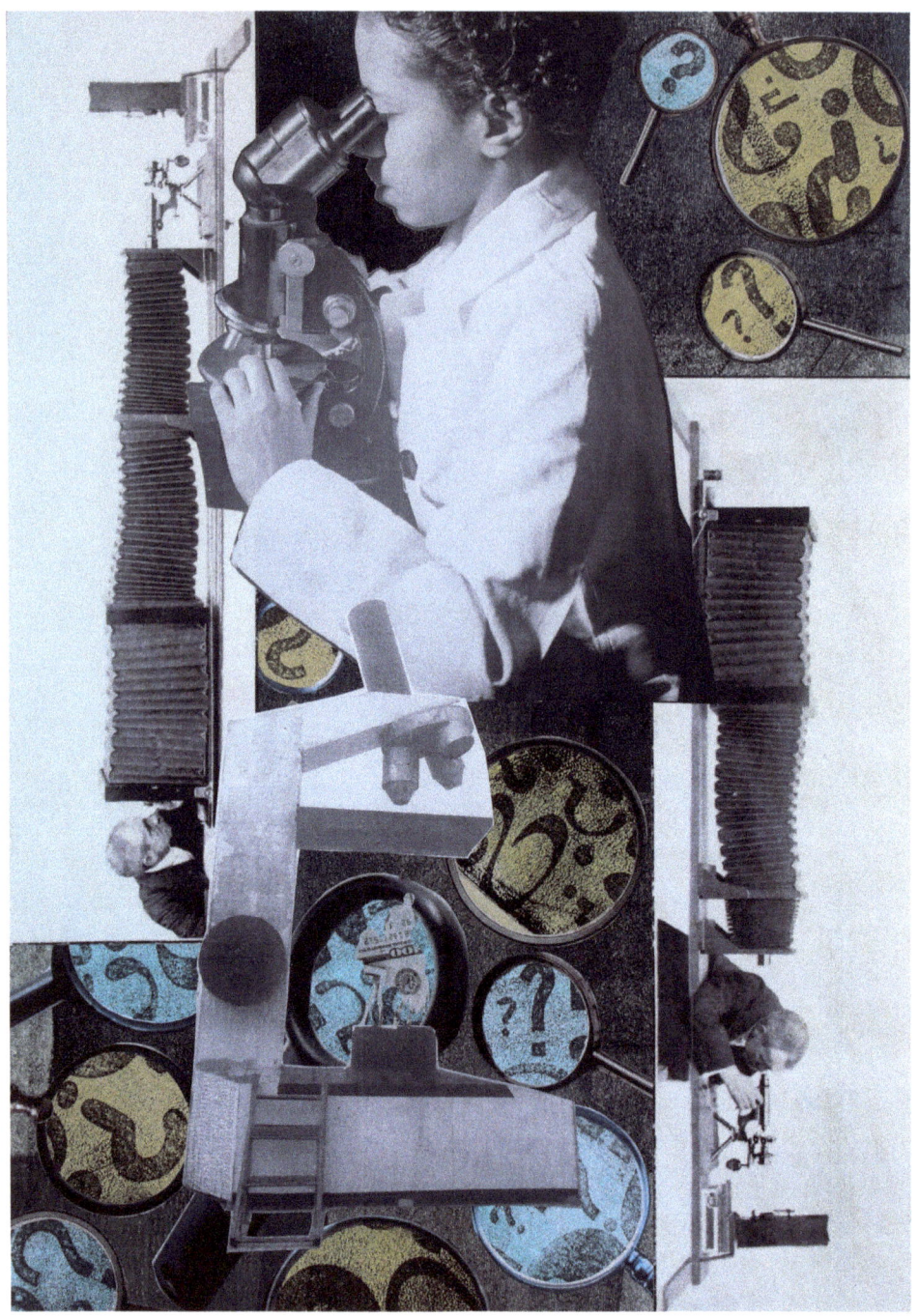

Finding Focus by Jennifer R Myhre

The artist wrote, "The center of this collage is an image from the Library of Congress of a black woman who is a lab tech in a hospital in the mid-1900s looking through a microscope. She is surrounded by tools for looking more closely at something. This collage is in conversation with the politics of outrage and the technique articulated by Steve Bannon of 'flooding the zone' and the difficulty of focusing on what matters. The key image in the collage is intentionally small—a silhouette of the famous image of a shirtless Putin on a horse cut out of 100 dollar bills. We need to follow the money but shock and awe politics make it difficult."

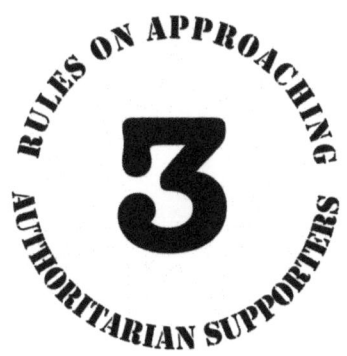

Focus on what you have in common.

Do you live in the same neighborhood?

Do you work in the same company or sector?

The smaller the community, the easier it is.

Give examples, like "we all need to get this done for all of us, if we don't cooperate neither of us will have it".

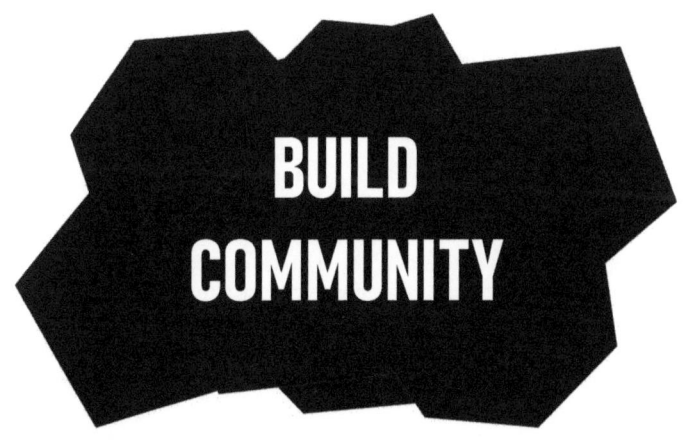

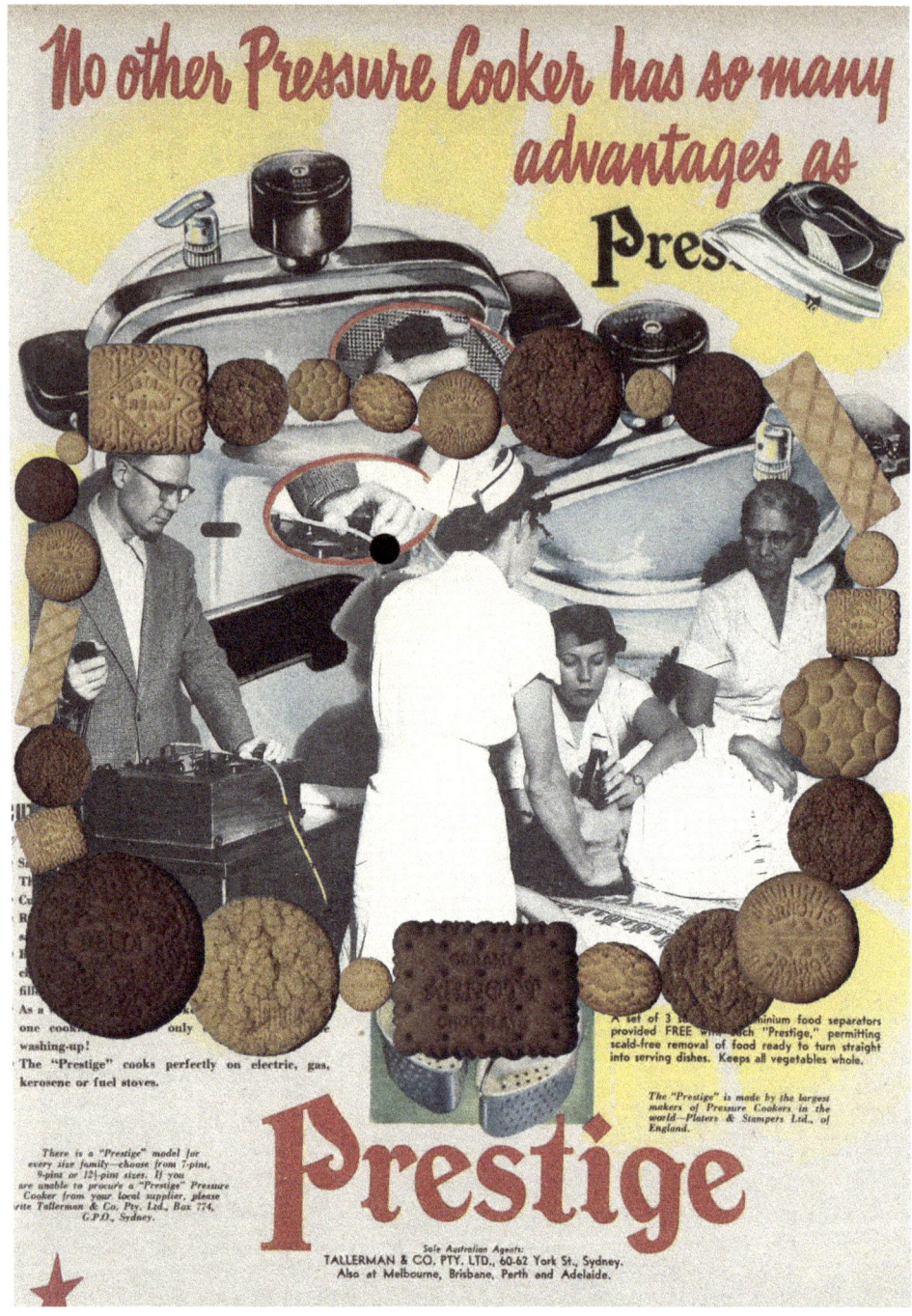

nostalgia (electroconvulsive) by Olivia Baldacci

"This work speaks to how authoritarianism historically targets women and their autonomy. This ranges from banning reproductive health services to endorsing sexual harassment," wrote the artist. "I want the viewer to think about how recent restrictions on reproductive health services are directly tied to a power grab by authoritarian states. The central black and white image is a photograph of electroconvulsive therapy from the late 1940s, set upon the background of a 1940s advertisement for pressure cookers. The frame is created by crackers and cookies from the 1940s and 1950s food advertisements."

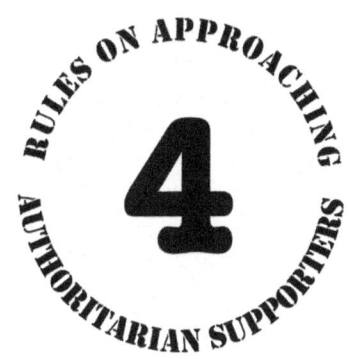

RULES ON APPROACHING AUTHORITARIAN SUPPORTERS

Use their language, don't treat it as inferior or below you – don't seem patronizing.

If they curse, curse with them. If they approach you with humor, don't get angry or uptight about it, reply with humor.

Show them you're actually not that different.

As long as you communicate on two different planes, you will never meet.

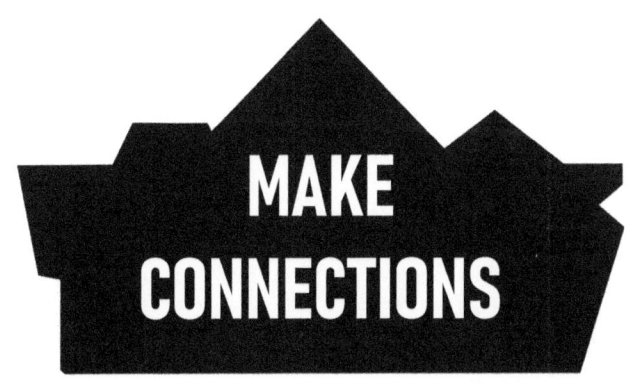

MAKE CONNECTIONS

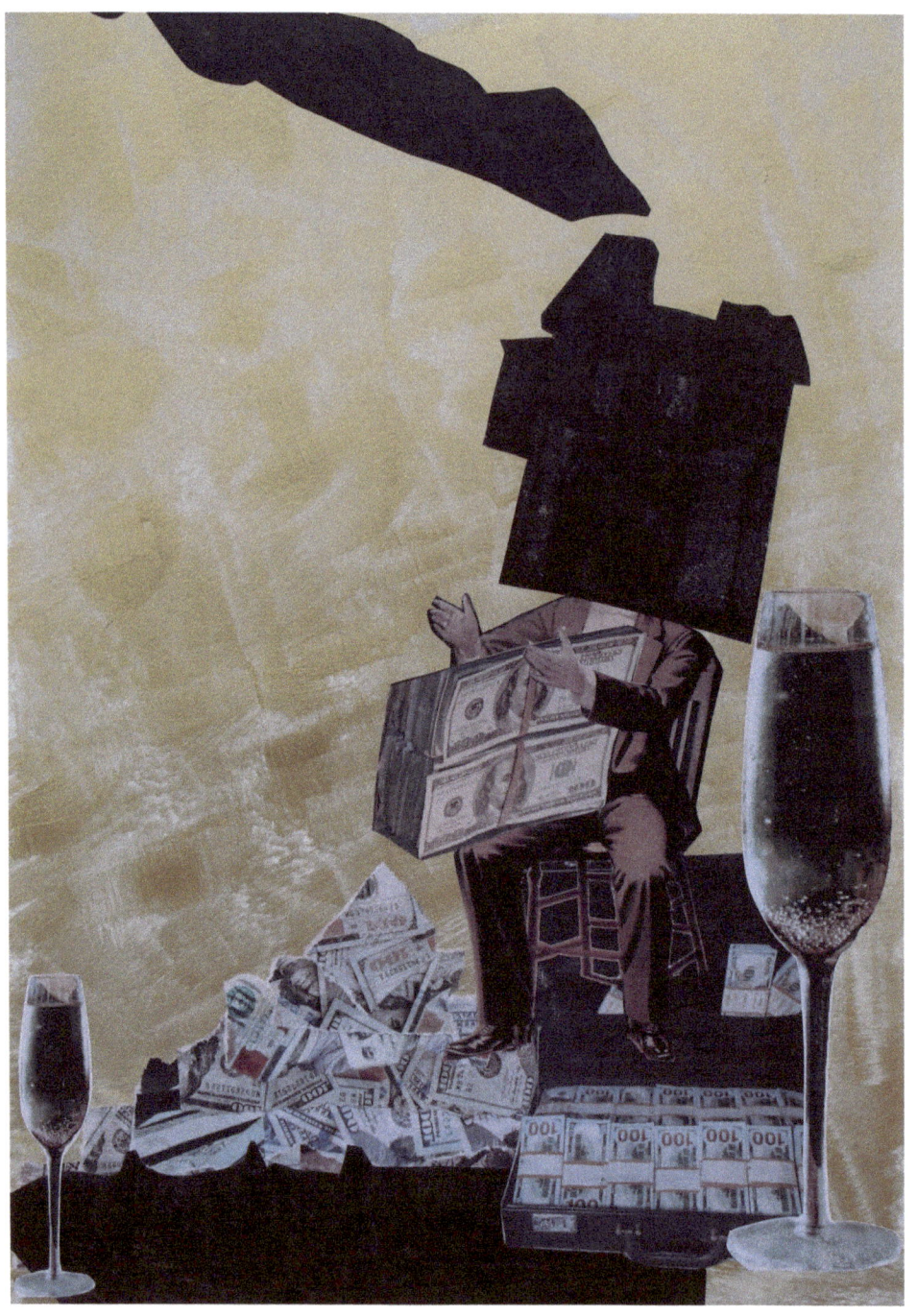

Champagne Dreams of the Oligarchs by Jennifer R Myhre
A faceless figure, a briefcase of cash, and a champagne glass is a picture of oligarchy. The artist wrote, "This collage connects the politics of death and destruction to the rise of oligarchs and the billionaire class, and asks the audience to consider how the drive to maximize wealth both rests on and results in large-scale suffering."

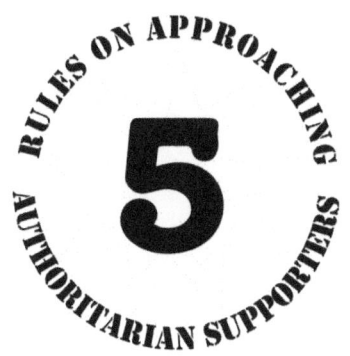

Don't block their news sources, don't turn away from their leaders and authority figures.

Treat them as an insight to their worldview and tactics.

Use them to your advantage, to better prepare for their arguments.

Whenever you don't agree with something or detect a lie, voice it calmly, expose it with factual arguments.

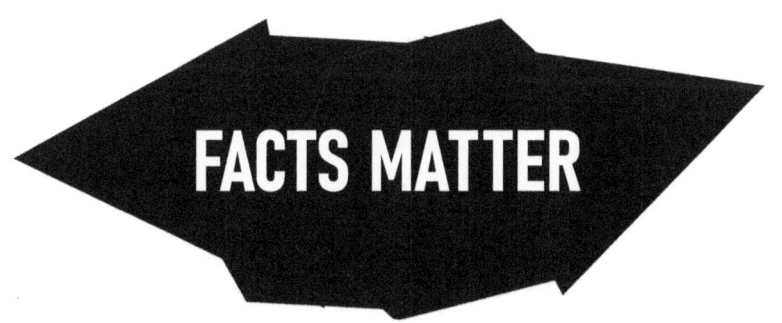

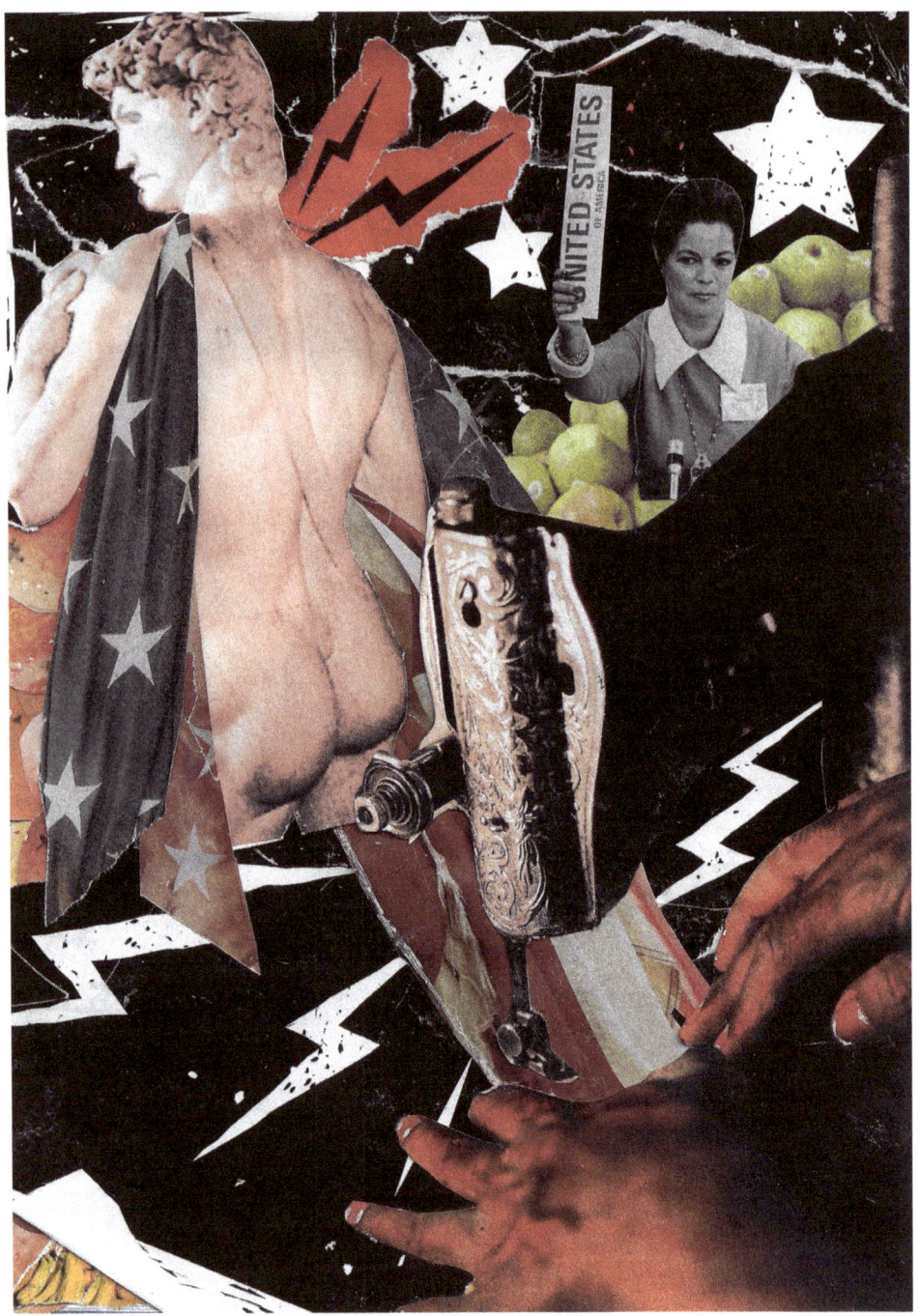

Sewing Division by Heather Wright

This surreal collage combines images of sewing, fruit, and sculpture to comment on the state of affairs. The artist wrote, "As dated as the sewing machine itself, the attempt to stitch the fabric of society with fascism by an authoritarian leader is so yesterday. The buttocks echo the idea of division and the flag draping the figure is being drawn into the stitch exposing its behind. The woman is trying to signal America-at-Risk but the division is creating apples vs oranges around the other figure and her. One may also view the apples as Americana. In the bottom left corner, one may spot bananas, because what is going on in the world right now is bananas."

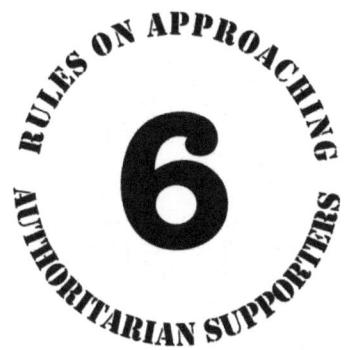

Pinpoint the practical, negative effects of their side's actions, ones that affect them directly.

Find examples of how they, their families, children or friends will be personally impacted by their policies, or how it will affect your shared community.

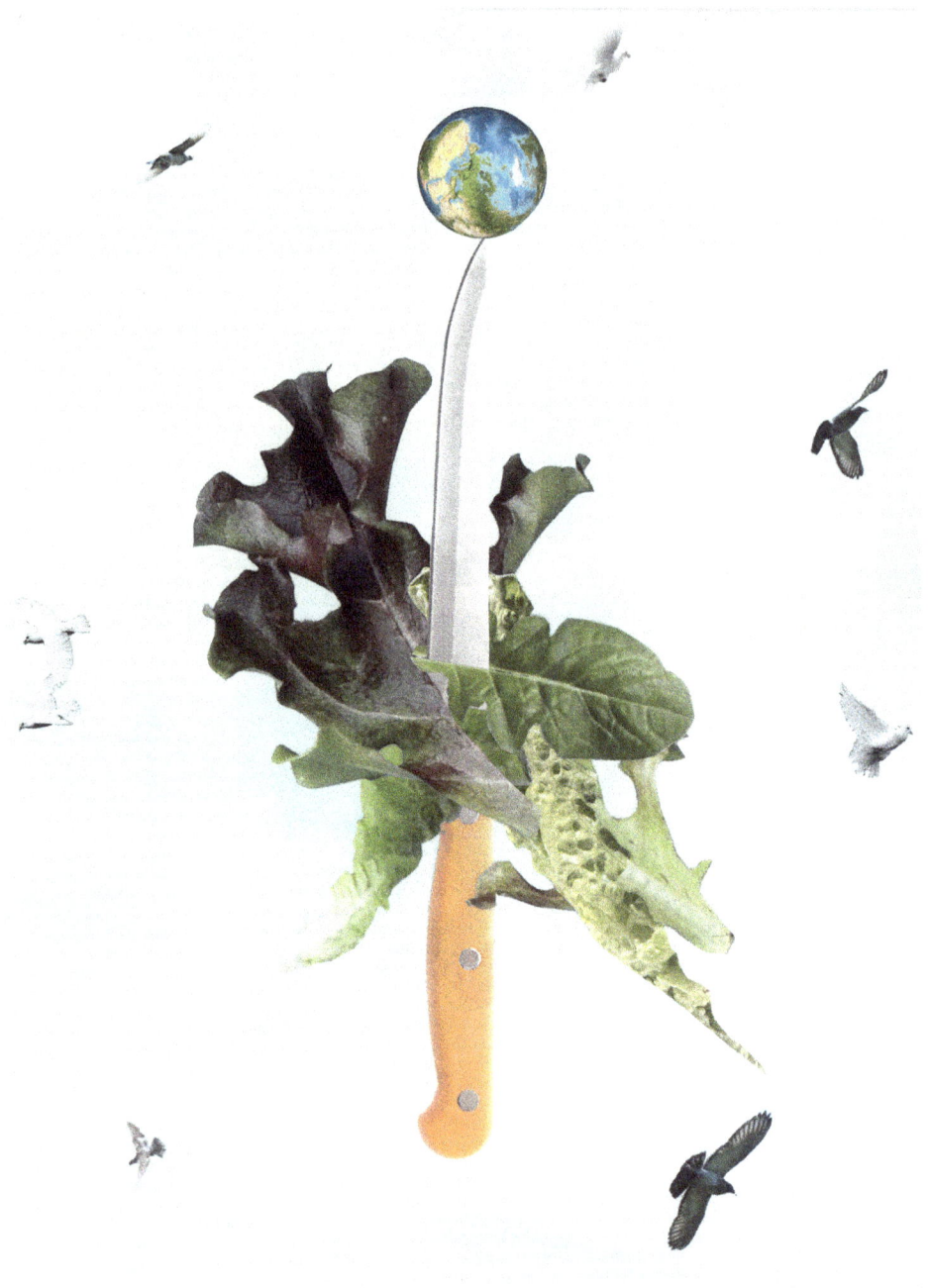

Lettuce Not Waver by Andrea Lee

"This work is an homage to John Heartfield's *The Meaning of Geneva. Where Capital lives, Peace cannot live!* (1932) in which a dove is seen impaled on a sword," wrote the artist. "Applying a post-modern lens to update the Heartfield work, a plastic kitchen knife is used in place of a sword as a commentary on how close to home the issues of authoritarianism have become. Birds taking off in various trajectories indicate prior knowledge. The shape and drape of the lettuce leaves memorializes the 1932 bird and reminds us of the violence that may yet to come, that there is much at stake, and that we should not waver in our commitment to stand strong."

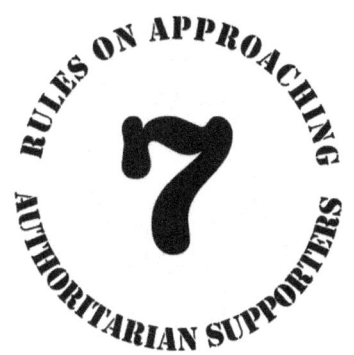

If all else fails, don't turn away, don't abandon your friends and family, don't shun your neighbors.

Remember, an authoritarian wants to divide you to control you.

So invite them over to your BBQ, crack open a beer, and who knows, maybe they'll realize you're not so different after all.

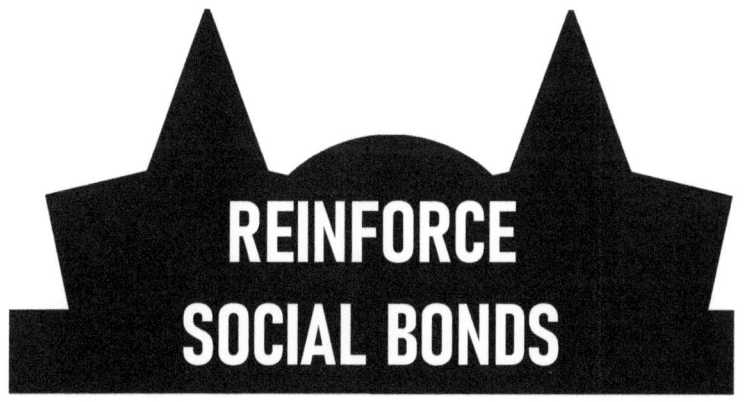

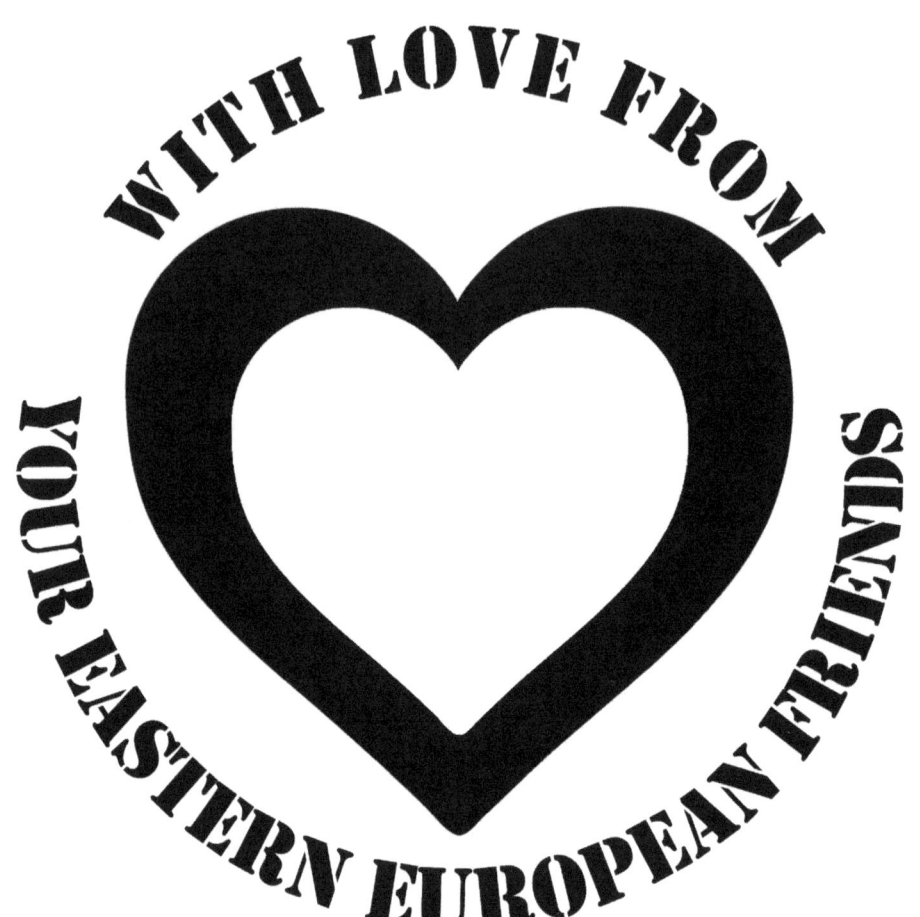

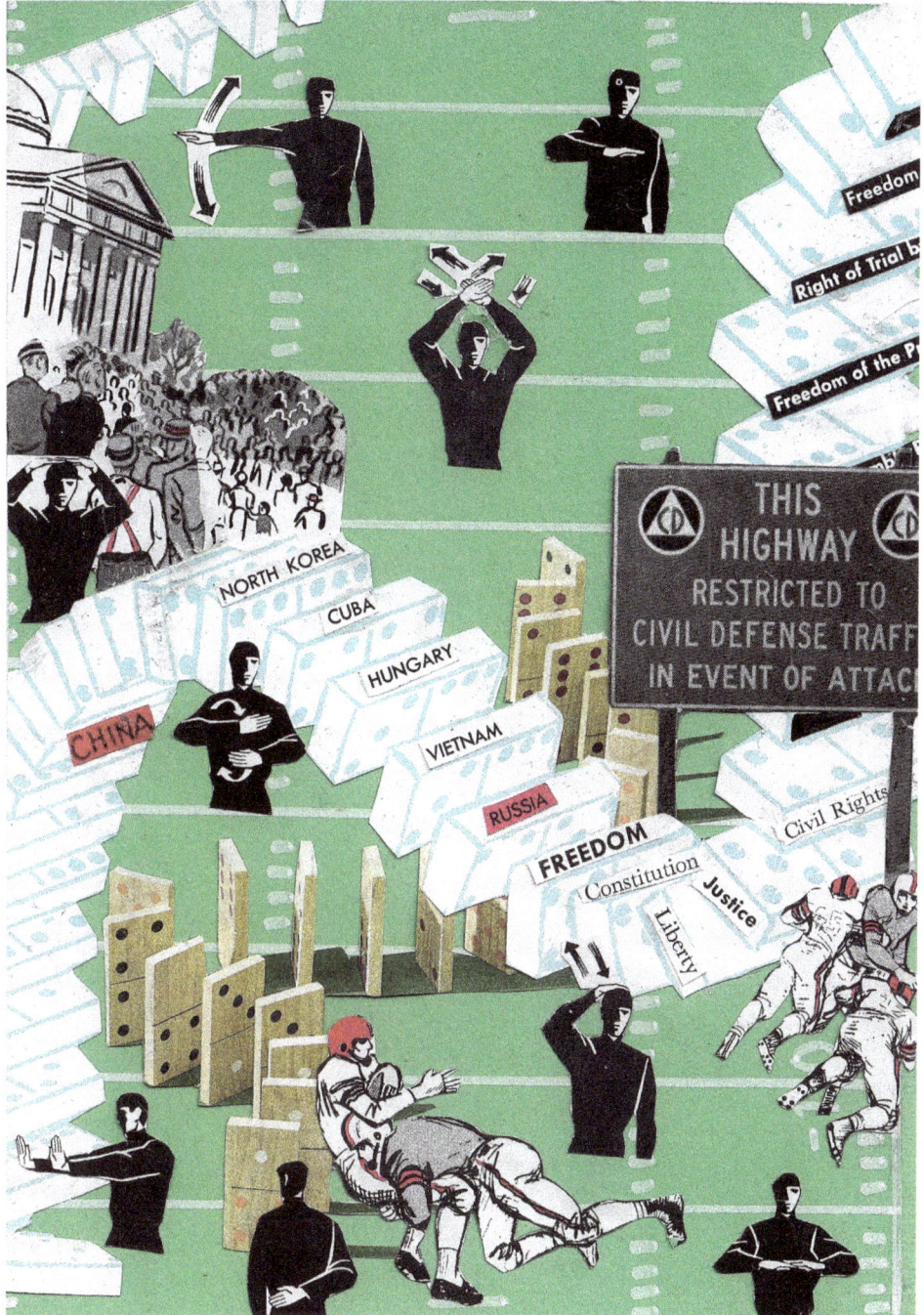

Flag on the Field by Heather Wright

The artist wrote, "Authoritarianism is on our home field. It has experienced players and plays dirty. All the refs are signaling illegal moves, but the game never takes a time out. We must do our best to stop the dominoes, other countries at risk, from falling. We ARE being attacked."

Authoritarian Regime Survival Guide by Martin Mycielski

Artwork by Olivia Baldacci, Suzanne Gore, Andrea Lee, Jennifer R Myhre, Lori Petchers, Heather Wishik, and Heather Wright.

Text © Martin Mycielski
Introduction Text © Ric Kasini Kadour
Images © the respective artists

Art Direction, Cover Design and Layout by Ric Kasini Kadour

Published by Kolaj Institute & Maison Kasini Canada
Printed in the USA

ISBN 978-1-927587-74-4
Legal deposit—Bibliothèque et Archives nationales du Québec, 2025
Legal deposit—Library and Archives Canada, 2025

All rights reserved. No part of this publication may be used or reproduced in any manner whatsoever without permission from the publisher. Infringement is liable to remedies rendered by the copyright act.

www.ingramcontent.com/pod-product-compliance
Lightning Source LLC
Chambersburg PA
CBHW040517220526
45473CB00012B/2898